introduction

Congratulations! You're about to embark on the adventure we call parenthood. Awaiting your new arrival is an exciting time, but one that can be frightening for any family on a budget. A walk through a baby superstore could leave any soon-to-be parent with a serious case of sticker shock. Whoever thought such a tiny creature would need so many things?

When my daughter was born in 1999, I stopped working full-time to become a stay-at-home mom. Money was tight, to say the least. Since I wasn't making as much money as I previously had, I decided that saving money would be my job. I read countless books and magazine articles, and visited Internet sites. I had always been thrifty by nature, but now I had to take it to a whole new level. I decided to share my knowledge with other parents by creating my own website. Thus, in April of 2000, Mommysavers.com was born.

Mommysavers.com began with a couple dozen pages, primarily just tips on how to save money on baby items and household expenses. Now it encompasses over a thousand pages on every aspect of frugality. In our community, parents support each other through discussion boards, shopping tips, articles, and a weekly newsletter.

This book is a collection of all the best money-saving baby advice that has been shared on the website and newsletter over the last ten years. With two little ones of my own and tips from hundreds of other moms, this book encompasses the best tried-and-true tips from *real* parents. Included are some great suggestions for do-it-yourself baby products, advice on what not to buy, and tips on how to find new things at rock-bottom prices.

The good news is that you *can* raise an infant on modest means without depriving yourself or your baby of anything. While retailers would have you believe otherwise, what babies need most is love, attention, and nurturing care, all of which are free. With a little time and creativity, any parent can learn to get by on

even the strictest budget. Financial struggles shouldn't get in the way of you enjoying your little one.

Have a question or comment regarding this book? Visit the website Mommysavers.com and post a message on our discussion board.

* PART ONE *

before your

baby
arrives

* chapter 1 *
the maternity months

things to think about now

1. Once you become pregnant, your doctor will prescribe prenatal vitamins. Even if you have a reasonable co-pay, they can be expensive. Look for generic over-the-counter prenatal vitamins at discount stores and pharmacies to save even more money.

2. Pregnancy books, workout videos, etc., are great to have, but don't pay full price for them.

They often wind up at secondhand stores, thrift shops, eBay, and consignment stores.

3. Better yet, borrow books and DVDs from the library before purchasing them. If you don't see what you want, request it via interlibrary loan.

FREE

4. Don't buy an expensive body pillow from a maternity store. Wal-Mart carries a full-length pillow for under $10. If you find it to be too overstuffed for your liking, just open a seam and remove some of the fiberfill.

5. Steer clear of expensive creams that say they can prevent or erase stretch marks. While they sound wonderful, they can't live up to their claims. Heredity gave you stretch marks, and no amount of

cream will erase them. On the upside, stretch marks do tend to fade with time.

6. Talk to your employer about the benefits you'll receive while on maternity leave. Some offer paid leave if you qualify. Most offer short-term disability for a short time after your baby is born, which is meant to cover your salary (or a portion of it) while you are unable to work due to illness or injury or childbirth.

7. Start stocking up on baby items now. If money is going to be tight after your little one arrives, start buying right away. For example, buy one pack of diapers for each paycheck you receive (just be sure not to buy too many of one size). This will ease the financial strain on your family once the baby comes.

8. Medicaid may pay for your prenatal care if you meet eligibility requirements. Medicaid is a health insurance program for certain individuals that is funded and administered through a State-Federal partnership. To find out if you meet eligibility requirements, contact your local or county medical assistance, welfare, or social services office. http://www.cms.hhs.gov/home/medicaid.asp

9. If your insurance doesn't fully cover your prenatal care and hospital stay, investigate using a Certified Nurse Midwife. A Certified Nurse Midwife is a registered nurse who has gone on to complete further training in childbirth situations, and is a safe alternative to an MD as long as you have a normal pregnancy without any complications. Many women claim their birth experience is more fulfilling with a midwife, and is far less costly than using a doctor and hospital.

http://www.midwife.org (United States)
http://www.canadianmidwives.org (Canada)

10. See if your hospital offers childbirth/ Lamaze and nursing classes to expectant parents. Most offer these courses free of charge to parents who will be giving birth there. Not only will you be gaining valuable information, you may form lasting friendships with other couples who will be going through the stages of parenthood at the same time you are.

FREE

11. In the last month before giving birth, stock your freezer with meals you can eat when your baby arrives. Once your baby is here, you won't have much time or energy to cook. Having meals at your disposal will prevent you from spending needlessly on take-out and convenience items.

have a baby shower!

12. Do have a baby shower! Don't feel guilty even if you have to ask a friend or family member to host one for you. Most are happy to do so. People who are invited to your shower would most likely want to give you a gift anyway, and this way they get to share in the celebration of your impending arrival.

WORTH IT

13. Don't hesitate to return unneeded items you receive at your shower. Your friends would want you to have what you wanted, and would hate to have something sit unused.

14. Be sure to register for gifts. A gift registry can serve as a guide to friends who want to buy you a gift but are unsure of your wants and needs. Most retailers will also offer you valuable coupons for baby products when you register. Having

a registry also makes things easier for you when you need to return unneeded items.

15. Ignore the "suggested" list the stores provide when you register. Most encourage you to buy much more than you actually will need. Talk to experienced mothers and find out what they think really is helpful and what is not.

16. Avoid registering for too many baby clothes. They're popular gift items, and you'll get more than enough without requesting any at all. By the time your baby arrives the clothing you've registered for may be on clearance, which means you won't get much back if you need to return them.

17. Consider Target's registry even if you don't expect friends and family to shop there. You'll get a 10 percent off completion coupon good for any items remaining in your registry, so add everything you think you may need to purchase. They'll also send you valuable store coupons to use (hint: these can be combined with manufacturer's coupons to save even more).

18. Don't request "theme" items. Unless you want to end up with a lampshade, outlet covers, and wall hangings adorned with Peter Rabbit, avoid telling friends and family which theme you've chosen. There are more practical ways to spend money.

19. If you don't need a lot of baby items or are unsure as to what you'll need, add gift cards to your registry. They will be handy to have later on as different needs arise.

20. Invite the guys, too. Invite *all* your friends, regardless of whether they're male or female. An outdoor grill-out or Sunday football bash may appeal to the men on your guest list. The hostess can tell them the only shopping requirement is to stop by and pick up a pack of diapers in any size.

21. Don't forget to request practical items like diapers, wipes, hand sanitizer, and formula. Even add them to your gift registry. Having these necessities on hand will free up your own money for future expenses.

22. Keep track of gifts you receive to make sending thank-you notes even easier. If possible, send as many as you can before your baby arrives. It's hard to find time to write them afterward.

23. Wait until *after* your shower to buy baby items. Until you receive the majority of your gifts, you really don't know what you will need. It is best to wait to make any major purchases.

24. Register online. If you only create one online registry, consider Amazon.com. Their site is linked with several different merchants, making adding items from several different websites using the universal "wish list" button extremely easy.

25. Don't forget to register for things to make your life as a parent easier and more comfortable. A new cordless phone, a digital camera, blank note cards for writing thank-you notes, scrap-books, photo albums, a handheld vacuum cleaner, or toiletries to pamper mom are all things you may wish for when your baby arrives.

26. Consider registering at other places that offer completion coupons. Babies "R" Us offers 10 percent off the total purchase of items left on your registry, baby registry announcements, invitations, and printable insert cards (announcing where you're registered). If you are registered there, you can return an item without a receipt. Pottery Barn Kids offers a 10 percent completion discount for any purchases off your registry for six months after your event date.

10% OFF

when the big day comes

27. Skip the photographs of your newborn that the hospital sells. These photos are very pricey (most packages start at $40) and are typically taken by a nurse, not a professional photographer. Instead, take your own photos in the hospital and wait two weeks to have a professional portrait taken at a studio. In a couple of weeks, your baby will have much more character and you'll pay a fraction of the cost of

the hospital pictures. Plus, you'll have your choice of backgrounds and props.

28. Bring your baby book to the hospital. The nurses can do your baby's footprints and handprints in it when they do them for his birth certificate. This saves you time and the cost of buying an ink kit to do it yourself later. *(FREE)*

29. When you go to the hospital, make sure you bring along your own ibuprofen to help manage the pain after birth. Hospitals sometimes charge quadruple the cost for most medications and you can save a lot of money by bringing your own.

30. Refuse anything you don't need. Remember that you're most likely paying for each pill, nursing pad, and sanitary item that the nurses give you.

31. Don't spend your money on expensive nightgowns or sleepwear for the hospital. The gowns the hospital provides are comfortable, great for nursing, and you won't have to worry if they get stained. Instead, purchase a robe to slip on when visitors come.

32. Once your bundle of joy arrives, you'll want to spread the news! Don't forget to bring your cell phone and charger so you don't end up having to use the hospital phone.

33. Bring along some snacks for you and your guests in the hospital. Vending machines are usually available, but can cost a lot of money.

34. Make your own Tucks pads by soaking a maxi-pad in witch hazel. You can even

put them in the freezer. The coolness is comforting to tender episiotomy sutures.

35. Call your insurance provider before entering the hospital to see exactly what will be covered in your hospital stay. Ask what supplemental pain medications and services are included with your plan, such as an anesthesiologist who administers an epidural. Some plans don't cover such things, so be sure you find out in advance.

36. If you're not going to be nursing your baby, ask the hospital for more formula. Your nurses are usually happy to give you *FREE* more samples before you leave.

37. Take the goodies in your baby's bassinet at the hospital along home with you as long as you've started to use them. Your insurance

company gets billed for them regardless of whether you take them home or not. This goes for toiletries for mom as well (the witch hazel pads, peri-bottle, tooth-paste, etc., are yours to take).

38. Save your sheets by placing a thin beach towel on your side of the bed. Postpartum mothers are leaky creatures. Not only will your breasts leak, you will be shedding your water weight through perspiration.

39. Be sure to review your bill carefully once it arrives to make sure you aren't charged for any goods or services you didn't receive. If you do find an error in your invoice, notify your insurance provider right away. Keep detailed documentation of any dealings you have with insurance companies, and write down the names of medical and billing person-nel with whom you speak.

40. Before you leave the hospital, find out if there is a toll-free number or hotline available for you to call with any medical questions. It may save you an unnecessary trip to the emergency room with your baby in the middle of the night.

clothing savings for mom-to-be

the skinny (or not-so-skinny) on maternity clothes

41. Instead of shopping exclusively at maternity shops, consider buying regular clothing in a size or two larger than you usually do. These pieces will be useful when you're in that not-quite-showing stage of pregnancy. The clothing will also be useful postpartum as you're losing that extra baby weight. Shop clearance racks for the best bargains.

42. Ask friends who have just had a baby if they're interested in selling their maternity clothing, especially if you know they're done having children. Most will be happy to help you out, and will be glad to find a new home for clothing they no longer need.

43. Look for loose-fitting dresses, babydoll tops, and skirts with elastic waistbands to wear while you're pregnant. These styles lend themselves well as maternity wear, and can often be found on sales racks at the end of the season. Plus, they can still be worn after you've had your baby.

44. Check department stores such as Kohl's, Sears, and JCPenney for maternity clothing. These stores offer regular-priced items, but you can occasionally find some great bargains on their clearance racks. Shop Kohl's during their Kohl's Days sales when a $50 purchase gives you $10 to spend later on.

$10 COUPON

45. It isn't necessary to purchase a maternity bra. Even though they claim to fit even as you change sizes, most don't. Regular bras with a little more support will do just fine.

46. A jogging bra is an inexpensive alternative to a maternity bra. Most contain spandex, which accommodates ever-changing sizes well. Some moms even claim they are comfortable to wear to bed when breasts are tender.

REUSE

47. Don't buy everything all at once. Start with items such as jeans, khaki pants, and basic shirts and add to your collection as needed.

48. If you're planning to have more kids and your budget is limited, avoid anything trendy. If you don't, you'll end up with an entire wardrobe of out-of-date maternity clothes the next time around.

REUSE

49. Garage sales can be a great source for inexpensive maternity wear. If you're at a garage sale that has newborn clothing, ask if they have maternity clothing as well. Sometimes the seller simply forgets to put it out.

50. Don't forget to look for maternity clothing in thrift shops like Goodwill and Savers. While selection is usually limited, you may find a few

bargains. While you're there, also look for plus-sized clothing or larger-sized clothing that can double as maternity wear.

51. Consider borrowing maternity clothing from friends who aren't pregnant at the same time you are. You can return the favor by lending them your maternity clothing the next time they need it.

FREE

52. When you buy new pieces, make sure they match the styles and colors you typically wore before becoming pregnant. Otherwise, you'll end up spending even more money on shoes, earrings, and other accessories.

53. Avoid buying maternity clothes that are too small. When trying on pieces you plan on wearing through the end of your pregnancy, use a belly pillow to make sure they will still fit later on.

54. Shop wisely. When buying at maternity retailers, be sure to inquire about their return policy. Many of them have strict policies that prevent customers from returning things after ten or fourteen days of purchase.

55. Look on Craigslist or your local paper's online classifieds section for gently used maternity clothes. Or, post a want ad.

56. Target offers some of the best bargains out there for maternity apparel. They even offer designs by Liz Lange (designer to fashion-conscious Hollywood moms). While their regular prices are great (hardly anything over $25), their sales are even better. It's not uncommon to find bargains marked down 30 percent, 50 percent, or even 75 percent on a regular basis. Their maternity clearance is not located in a separate section, so be prepared to look through the regular ladies' clearance racks. If your Target has a limited maternity assortment, shop their online store.

75% OFF

57. Wal-Mart and Kmart offer maternity wear at reasonable prices. They have a good selection of basics like jeans and tees that can be dressed up with your own shoes and accessories. Hardly anything is over $25, and they also offer clearance merchandise.

58. Shop factory outlet stores for maternity wear. Visit www.outletbound.com for a listing of maternity outlets in your state or area.

59. Motherhood Maternity, a popular boutique for maternity wear, has over seventy outlet stores across the United States. While their outlet prices are comparable to their regular stores, you can often find great deals in the back of the store on their clearance racks.

60. While The Gap doesn't stock maternity apparel in each of their regular stores, most of their outlet stores offer a very small selection of maternity clothing. Look in the rear of the store near the baby/layette department. You are likely to find a couple of styles of pants and/or blouses available at outlet pricing.

61. Most Old Navy stores offer maternity clothing in-store. They also sometimes stock returns from their online maternity department. Check the clearance racks of their bricks-and-mortar stores for any maternity clothing that has been returned.

62. Shop The Gap and Old Navy midweek. That's when they do their markdowns, and by beating the weekend crowd you'll get the best selection of clearance items.

63. Consignment stores may also carry maternity wear. Consult your yellow pages to see if there are any consignment stores in your area, and give them a call before stopping by.

64. Stores that sell gently used baby items, such as Once Upon a Child and Kid to Kid, may also stock maternity clothing. Call before you go, as not all of their locations carry maternity wear. For a listing of stores in your area, visit them online at www.ouac.com and www.kidtokid.com.

buy online and save

65. Sign up for deal alerts at your favorite online retailers, or hit several of them all at once by visiting www.shopittome.com. Creating an account is free, and you can sign up for email alerts when your favorite maternity brands go on sale in your size.

66. Some of your favorite retailers also carry maternity sizes online. Retailers like the Ann Taylor Loft, Lands' End, and The Gap offer a small selection of maternity clothing online comparable to the quality and price of their nonmaternity apparel.

Many moms-to-be like it because the styles compare to what they would be wearing if they weren't pregnant.

67. EBay is a great source for maternity clothes. Look for groups or "lots" of clothing to save even more money. Be sure to note the condition of the clothes you're buying, and pay close attention to the seller's feedback rating. Ask any questions about sizing prior to placing your bid, since you won't be able to try them on before buying.

68. EBay is also a great place to look if you're dressing up for a formal occasion. You'll likely find dozens of dress options in your size that are just a fraction of what something new would cost. Chances are it's only been worn once or twice, so you're getting a great value. Plus, you can recoup your investment by reselling it when you're done!

69. Maternitymall.com is a portal for several maternity clothing brands offering their goods online. Stores like Motherhood Maternity, A Pea in the Pod, and Destination Maternity can all be accessed. Click on the "sale" tabs to view clearance merchandise at up to 75 percent off.

75% OFF

70. Even if you have a Wal-Mart, Kmart, or Target in your area, you may find a larger selection of maternity apparel online. Wal-Mart even offers $0.97 shipping, which may cost less than the gas to get you to their bricks-and-mortar store. Target usually offers free shipping over a certain dollar amount (such as $50).

71. Most maternity apparel sites include a "Sale" or "Clearance" area of their site in which to look for bargains. Among them:

* www.motherhood.com—Click on "Sale" to save up to 60 percent or more.

* www.onehotmama.com—Click on "Hot Deals" to save 50 percent or more.

* www.momshop.com—Click on "Clearance" to browse their markdowns.

* www.japaneseweekend.com—Includes both sale and clearance sections.

* www.kikisfashions.com—Check out their "Under $10" and clearance sections.

* www.duematernity.com—Great for organic clothing and nursing wear. Click on their "Sale" tab.

72. Try a bartering board for maternity clothing. Mommysavers.com has a bartering board where parents can trade goods and services without having money change hands. Post your request by visiting this link: www.mommysavers.com.

73. Old Navy also offers a wide selection of maternity clothes online. They also have a "bargains" section of their website devoted to maternity wear.

74. Buy with online coupon codes to save even more money. You can find the best bargains by combining clearance items with free shipping and online coupon codes. Sites like www.retailmenot.com and www.fatwallet.com are good places to look.

75. Special event consignment sales are another great place to search for maternity clothing. Just Between Friends is a popular resale event franchise. Visit their website to look for sales in your area: www.jbfsale.com.

76. Look for gift cards for your favorite maternity and clothing retailers for sale online for less than their face value. For example, you may be able to purchase a $100 gift card for $80. Sites to check out include www.cardavenue.com and eBay.

other options

77. Drawstring pants work well as maternity wear. They can be adjusted as you grow and can be used after the baby is born when you're trying to shed those extra pounds. Yoga pants and lounge pants stretch, and can also be worn under your belly.

REUSE

7.8. To save money on maternity clothing, raid your husband's closet (assuming, of course, that he's bigger than you). Loose-fitting items such as T-shirts, sweaters, and sweatshirts will look just fine, even if you have to push up the sleeves. Adding feminine accessories such as necklaces or scarves will take off the masculine edge.

BORROW

79. At under $30, the Belly Band is a good investment. It's a tube of stretchy fabric designed to cover your regular pants when you can't zip them up that also holds up maternity pants that may still be too big. It can help extend your wardrobe during pregnancy and postpartum and help you avoid spending too much on maternity clothes.

WORTH IT

80. Avoid having to buy maternity panty hose by wearing your regular hose and rolling or folding down the waist to just under your belly. You

can also wear longer dresses and pantsuits with thigh-high or knee-high hose, or skip the hose altogether.

81. Look for low-rise jeans instead of maternity jeans. Your ever-expanding belly won't be constrained by a waistband, allowing room for growth.

82. Maternity underwear isn't necessary. Bikini underwear works well because it rests under your belly, not over it. Save your money for attractive lingerie when you're not pregnant anymore.

83. Do invest in accessories you can wear later. A new pair of earrings, a scarf, or a fun handbag can help make you feel more put-together when your wardrobe isn't what it used to be. Accessories also help dress up basic clothing and keep you looking stylish and up-to-date.

WORTH IT

84. Many people's feet swell during pregnancy, especially during the hot summer months. Instead of purchasing an expensive pair of shoes, buy flip-flops or other slip-ons. Not only are they less expensive, they allow more room for feet to expand. Plus, you don't even have to bend over to tie them!

85. If you know how to sew, instructions for adapting regular clothes into maternity styles can be found online.

86. Turn your regular pants into maternity pants by safety-pinning a strip of elastic onto the waistband (a hair elastic works well looped through the button hole of your jeans and hooked onto the button). Your maternity tops should be long enough to cover the fly area anyway, and no one will ever know the difference. The solution isn't permanent, so you can go back to using your pants normally after the baby is born.

REUSE

⁎ chapter 3 ⁎

bargains
for multiple
bundles

twins, triplets, and more

87. Join a twins or multiples group. Not only will the other parents provide valuable moral support, you'll get a lot of great ideas on saving money from your network of parents.

88. Don't fall into the trap of buying two of everything (swings, bouncy chairs, toys, etc.). You will need two of certain items (car seats, for example) but not items like toys. Be sure to think

through each purchase to determine whether or not you'll really need more than one.

89. You may not need two cribs. Many parents of twins find that their babies not only enjoy sharing a crib, but prefer it. You may be wise to wait until your babies are older to see if you'll need to buy an additional crib.

90. Instead of buying two bath seats for your tub, use two inexpensive laundry baskets. The baskets fit well in the tub, one behind the other. Babies sit in a smaller amount of water and are more contained. When they're ready for the big tub, you can use the baskets for laundry.

(REUSE)

91. Feed with one bowl and one spoon if no one is sick. This is so much easier than feeding with two spoons and two bowls.

92. Save time when making large batches of formula by using a pitcher. Make enough for a day's supply, and either store the pitcher in the fridge or pour directly into bottles.

93. Check into which multiples groups in your area have rummage sales. Some offer early shopping to mothers of multiples.

freebies for multiples!

94. Contact any company whose products you use (by calling the toll-free number on the product packaging) and ask if they have a multiples program. The worst they can do is say no, and in most cases they'll at least mail you some good coupons to use.

95. Many formula companies participate in multiple birth programs, but require a referral from your OB-GYN or pediatrician. The next time you're at an appointment, ask your caregiver to fill out a Multiple Birth Referral Form for you to photocopy and mail to various companies.

96. Beechnut Food Corporation will send parents of multiples coupons and information on their label saving program if you call their toll-free number, 1-800-BEECHNUT (1-800-233-2468).

97. Heinz (Nature's Goodness baby food) offers free welcome packets for each of your twins or triplets. The packs also include coupons for Heinz baby products. Call 1-800-USA-BABY (1-800-872-2229).

FREE

98. Gerber also has a multiple birth program. Contact them at 1-800-4-GERBER (1-800-443-7237) for baby food, coupons, spoons, etc.

99. Huggies offers coupons for diapers and wipes to parents of multiples. You'll need to provide copies of the birth certificates and mail them to:

U.S. Requests:
Kimberly-Clark Corporation
Department QMB
PO Box 2020
Neenah, WI 54957-2020

Canadian Requests:
Kimberly-Clark, Inc.
Department QMB
50 Burnhamthorpe Road West
Mississauga, ON L5B 3Y5

100. Participate in the Luvs Multiple Birth Offer by mailing your name and address along with copies of the hospital discharge papers to:

Luvs Multiple Birth Offer
The Procter & Gamble Company
P.O. Box 599
Cincinnati, OH 45201

101. Contact Sassy Baby Products at 1-800-323-6336 for offers, which vary, or write to:

Sassy Baby Products
2305 Breton Industrial Park Dr. SE,
Kentwood, MI 49508

102. Babies "R" Us offers a 10 percent discount to parents of multiples when they purchase two or more of the same products in the same order. The discount pertains to the following categories only: furniture, bedding sets, and baby gear. For more details, visit your nearest Babies "R" Us store.

10% OFF

103. Parents of twins or triplets can receive a special assortment of Ocean Spray product coupons in the Multiple Birth program. Send a copy of proof of birth of your multiples to:

Ocean Spray Cranberries, Inc.
Consumer Affairs Department
One Ocean Spray Drive
Lakeville-Middleboro MA 02349

104. The First Years has a multiple birth program open to parents of twins, triplets, or higher number multiples. You'll receive free gifts from their current product lines. Contents may vary, but past gifts have included bibs, rattles, teethers, and toys. Just send photocopies of your children's birth certificates to:

FREE

Learning Curve Brands
Attn: Multiple Birth Program
2021 9th St. SE
Dyersville, IA 52040

* PART TWO *

feeding your

newborn
baby

breast-feeding

your own milk is healthy—and free!

105. Did you know that formula can cost $2,000 a year or more? Breast-feeding is far cheaper and is healthier for your baby. Plus, breast milk is always ready and available at the perfect temperature. It contains all the vitamins and minerals that your baby needs and provides an irreplaceable bonding experience for mother and child.

106. Breast-feeding also helps save on healthcare expenses. Studies show breast-fed babies are less likely to suffer from allergies, asthma, ear infections, gastroenteritis, and juvenile diabetes. This means they need fewer doctor visits and are hospitalized less often than their formula-fed counterparts. For working mothers, that means an added savings of less time lost on the job.

107. It's not all-or-nothing. Even nursing your baby once or twice a day will save money on formula. Your breasts will adapt to whatever feeding schedule you and your baby establish.

108. If you have trouble breast-feeding, consult a lactation nurse. Most breast-feeding problems are common and can be worked through. Many hospitals offer this service for free. If a lactation consultant isn't available to you, contact La Leche League. Check your phone book to see if your hometown has a local branch, or visit their website at: www.lalecheleague.org.

FREE

109. Breast-feeding provides health benefits for mom, too. Studies show that mothers who breast-feed are less likely to suffer from postpartum depression and certain forms of cancer. It also helps her get the baby weight off faster.

110. By exclusively breast-feeding, chances are you won't have a period until you've weaned your baby. Not only are you saving money on formula, you're not having to buy feminine hygiene products either.

111. Most moms experience a period where demand for milk exceeds supply. This can be remedied by drinking water, eating products made of oats, and pumping in between feedings to stimulate supply. Check with your lactation consultant or La Leche League for other methods of improving milk supply.

112. It's not too late! Most women assume that if they didn't start nursing right away or if they allowed their milk to dry up they can't go back. In some cases, relactation is a possibility. Don't rule it out, especially if your baby develops problems such as reflux in which you would have to purchase expensive formulas. Consult your doctor or lactation nurse to see if relactation is a possibility for you.

nursing apparel and accessories

113. C-shaped nursing pillows, such as the Boppy, are nice but not necessary. Simply propping your arms up on a couple of pillows should do the trick nicely. If you decide you want a Boppy, search for one at a thrift store, consignment store, eBay, or even make your own.

114. Nursing stools elevate your lap to help comfortably position you and your baby for nursing. However, their slanted design makes them impractical for use after you're no longer nursing. Instead, purchase a sturdy wooden step stool your child can use later.

115. Invest in at least two or three good nursing bras if you plan on breast-feeding for more than a couple of months. Your breasts change shape and size through different stages of nursing, so you'll need the added support. Choose one in 100 percent cotton and that isn't too tight to avoid problems like thrush and clogged milk ducts.

WORTH IT

116. Wait until late in pregnancy (the last month, preferably) to purchase a nursing bra. At this point your breasts will be closest to the size they will be while nursing. Don't buy more than one until after your milk comes in. You won't know what size you'll need until then.

117. Check discount retailers for nursing bras. Both Target and Wal-Mart have inexpensive nursing bras in the $10 to $12 range that hold up fairly well.

118. Sports bras can be used as nursing bras and are especially comfortable at night. Also, if you can't find a nursing bra you are happy with, you can always pull a regular bra up or down.

REUSE

119. Skip the nursing cape. Bring a blanket with you wherever you go; that way you can cover up regardless of what you're wearing. If you're on the go, places like fitting rooms, bathrooms, or even your car can give you the privacy you crave while nursing.

120. You will find that clothing designed specifically for nursing isn't necessary. Most of your regular clothing will work just fine.

121. If you want to buy clothing that's more functional for nursing, purchase regular button-down shirts or loose-fitting blouses. If the shirt is a little loose and on the long side there is enough material there to still keep you covered. Choose patterns in dark colors to hide leaks, spit-up, and other inevitable messes that come with nursing a baby.

122. Men's button-down shirts work well for nursing. Borrow some from your husband's closet.

123. If you're more comfortable wearing nursing apparel, buy some inexpensive tees or turtlenecks to wear under sweaters or blouses. Purchase them on clearance and cut slits in them yourself (you need to stitch around the openings so they won't unravel over time). You can also wear the T-shirts under sweaters and that keeps you completely

covered. Or, wear a cardigan sweater or a jacket. You can nurse in a regular shirt and easily stay covered up.

124. Disposable breast pads are convenient, but are costly. Instead, purchase a few pairs of machine-washable cotton breast pads that can be used over and over again.

125. Make your own breast pads. Be sure to use fabric that is 100 percent cotton (your husband's old T-shirts work well), allowing your skin to breathe. Cut several layers of circles and stitch an X through all the layers to keep them in place. To finish, zigzag or serge the round edge.

REUSE

126. Pantyliners cut in half can double as disposable breast pads. They are just as absorbent but cost much less.

127. A disposable diaper cut into circles can also be used as a breast pad. This is a great way to use up diapers your baby has outgrown.

REUSE

128. A baby can nurse comfortably and discreetly in a baby sling. While a new one may cost up to $40, it may be worth the investment. Or, sew one yourself for a fraction of the price. Simply enter search terms "free + baby + sling + pattern" for online instructions. By sewing one yourself, you get to customize the fabric and style.

129. If you sew, look for free patterns and tutorials for making your own nursing apparel online. Two of the best sites are www.elizabethlee.com and www.kellymom.com.

130. Switch to pajamas. It's much easier to pull up a pajama top than to unbutton a nightgown in the middle of the night. If you are used to wearing nightgowns and can't make the switch, take a couple of your older ones and cut slits in the side seams for nursing. You can stitch them back up when you're done nursing, or simply toss them out.

131. Look on eBay for nursing apparel. You may find gently used or even new nursing items at great savings.

132. Sites that sell maternity clothing (see chapter 2 for suggestions) usually offer nursing apparel as well. Search the bargains areas of their websites to find the best deals.

breast milk storage, pumps, and accessories

133. It isn't necessary to purchase special breast milk storage bags or containers. Pour breast milk into ice cube trays and freeze. When frozen, pop them out and store them in one-gallon freezer bags.

FREE

134. Pour your milk directly into smaller-sized ziplock bags. This method makes thawing and use a little easier. When it comes time for use, thaw and snip the corner off one side of the bag. Pour right into the bottle!

135. When deciding on a breast pump, consider how much you'll be using it. If you're returning to work and pumping every day, invest in a hospital-grade pump. If you'll only be using

it for the occasional bottle-feeding, you can get by with spending much less.

136. An electric breast pump can be expensive, but is worth the money if you'll be using it on a daily basis. The Medela Pump In Style model is highly recommended, which can retail for up to $300. It is an electric-powered double pump that allows you to empty both breasts quickly and at the same time. Manual or battery-operated breast pumps are much cheaper, but are extremely time consuming and don't work nearly as well.

WORTH IT

137. If you purchase your pump through a hospital, your insurance provider may cover part of the cost. Medicaid allows for a free breast pump for moms who need to go back to work or school.

138. Most hospitals will rent breast pumps for about $30/month. If you're going to be breast-feeding for more than a couple months it is more economical to buy a new pump and resell it when you're done, especially if you'll be using it for more than one child.

139. EBay is also a source for new, high-quality breast pumps. Be sure to look for a reputable seller with a high feedback rating.

140. Borrow a pump from a friend or look for a good used pump at a consignment store or on eBay. Don't be squeamish about buying a used pump. Purchase the pump only, and buy new attachments for it. The breast milk never touches the pump itself anyway.

141. Most breast-feeding moms fall victim to cracked or sore nipples, especially when they first start out nursing. Lanolin creams for dry and cracked nipples work well, but are extremely expensive. Breast milk itself is a natural healing agent. Rub a little milk on your nipples and allow them to air-dry for ten minutes.

FREE

142. If you do develop clogged milk ducts, try a warm compress. However, you don't have to purchase a hot water bottle or heating pad. Taking a hot shower works well, as does inserting a warm tea bag under your breast pad. Even soaking a clean diaper in warm water and using it as a hot compress works well.

FREE

formula, milk, and bottles

if you choose formula

143. If you're going to be using formula instead of breast-feeding, buy the powdered kind. While it may be more handy, the ready-to-feed varieties cost about double the price per ounce.

144. Prices for formula may vary within the same chain. For example, one discount retailer may sell its Similac for one price while another store twenty miles away sells it for a bit more. Be sure to check all stores (or better yet, call) in your area to compare prices.

WORTH IT

145. Join formula manufacturer's mailing lists to receive valuable offers by mail. Not only will you receive free samples, you will get coupons and retail checks good to purchase full cans of formula.

FREE

146. Similac StrongMoms Club—www.similac.com

147. When you enroll in Similac's StrongMoms Club, you'll receive newsletters containing pregnancy and parenting

advice, tips, and special offers that may include money-saving discounts, formula samples, or other gifts.

148. Enfamil Family Beginnings Club—www.enfamil.com

149. Enroll in the Enfamil Family Beginnings Club to receive lots of freebies and offers such as a diaper bag and changing pad, coupons for portrait sittings, and retail checks for formula. Customers can also enter the numbers on their formula cans to earn rewards points good for prize drawings and sweepstakes.

150. Gerber's Start Healthy Stay Healthy Club—www.gerber.com

151. Sign up for a free subscription to receive valuable retail checks for Nestle Good Start formula.

152. Store-brand formulas such as Parent's Choice from Wal-Mart are just as nutritionally sound as name-brand formulas. By law, all formula manufacturers have to adhere to the same FDA guidelines. So, by purchasing a cheaper brand, you don't have to worry that you're skimping on nutrition.

153. Formulas containing DHA (docosahexaenoic acid) and ARA (arachidonic acid) cost more than those that don't. Research to support their benefits is mixed, so you may want to question your urge to splurge for formulas that contain them.

154. When deciding which can of formula to buy, figure the cost per ounce of the formula when it's prepared, not the cost per ounce of the powder itself. Cans and scoop sizes can vary, making it difficult to compare prices directly.

155. Ask your pediatrician for formula samples when you're there for your well-baby checkup. Most offices have an abundance of samples and are happy to share them with you if you ask.

FREE

156. Formula coupons can be purchased off eBay for about half of their face value. This is especially helpful if your baby requires a special type of formula such as Alimentum or Nutramigen. Be sure to check the seller's feedback rating and find out what the expiration dates of the coupons are.

157. Cans of formula itself are auctioned off on eBay, too. Before bidding, make sure you know what the expiration date on the can is. Also, be sure to figure the cost of shipping in your bid.

158. Amazon.com is another not-so-well-known source for baby formula. They offer the large economy-sized cans, often at prices less than Target or Wal-Mart. As an added bonus, they often offer free shipping on qualifying orders.

159. Check the damaged section of your local grocery store for formula. You may save 25 to 50 percent on a can that has a little dent. However, never purchase a can that has been opened.

160. If your baby needs a specialized formula for medical reasons such as reflux or allergies, you can try to get your insurance provider to cover the cost. Prescriptions can be written for formulas; be sure to ask your doctor for details.

161. If your insurance doesn't cover the cost of specialized formulas, call the manufacturer. Many of them have "helping hands" programs that provide discounts or free formula cans to families in need.

162. See if you qualify for WIC. The Special Supplemental Nutrition Program for Women, Infants, and Children—better known as the WIC Program—serves to safeguard the health of low-income women, infants, and children up to age five. Applicants must meet eligibility criteria based on income and nutritional risk. For more information and

to see if you qualify, visit their website at http://www.fns.usda.gov/wic/.

163.

Use a funnel to get the last bit of formula out of the can. There is usually enough powder left in the bottom of the can to make an extra ounce or two.

164.

The biggest waste of money is "nursery water" that is promoted for use with baby formula. A gallon can cost as much as $2. Don't fall victim to this marketing ploy! The water your family uses for drinking should be safe for baby as well.

FREE

165.

In a pinch, formula can be made at home. However, even when made properly it is still inferior to breast milk and formula.

Check with your pediatrician before introducing this to your baby.

   2 12-ounce cans evaporated milk

   32 ounces water (boiled and cooled)

   2 tablespoons corn syrup

   3 milliliters Poly-Vi-Sol vitamins

   Mix thoroughly before serving.

166. Travel-sized packets of formula are convenient and great to stick in your diaper bag. Just tear off the end, pour into the bottle, and add water. However, they get to be expensive if you use them a lot. Instead, purchase a formula dispenser for around $4 in the baby section of Target or Wal-Mart. These little containers allow you to pour a premeasured amount of formula in your baby's bottle mess-free.

167. Premeasure your own powdered formula into those zippered snack-size baggies. It only takes a few minutes to prepare a few bags and you can carry a small pair of scissors to snip off the end to pour into the baby bottle (a small funnel may help too).

moving on to milk

168. By the age of twelve months, most babies can move directly on to whole milk with their pediatrician's approval. Formulas designed for older babies or toddlers are costly and unnecessary.

169. If you have unopened cans of formula you can't use, consider donating them to a food shelf. Not only will you be doing something to help others, you can claim your donation as a tax deduction (be sure to ask for a receipt).

170. Don't throw away open cans of formula. Instead, use the leftover formula in cooking or as a coffee creamer.

171. Save your receipts if you stock up on formula. Cans that are unopened and haven't passed their expiration date can be returned to the store.

172. Reuse baby formula scoops for dry ingredients in the kitchen, such as spices, coffee, baking soda, and so on. Your baby can use them as sandbox toys or for bathtub play.

REUSE

173. If you receive fancy silver baby spoons as a gift, reuse them to serve condiments when entertaining.

REUSE

best bets on baby bottles

174. Place nipples and tops of your bottles in a basket in your dishwasher so that they don't fall out and get burned by the heating element. You can make your own basket by using two green berry baskets from the produce department and attaching them with a twist tie.

175. When shopping for bottles, consider spending a little more and buying BPA-free plastic. BPA acts as an environmental estrogen and can leach from the plastic into liquids, especially when heated. Another safe option is to use glass bottles.

WORTH IT

176. Skip the small four-ounce bottles. It won't be long before you'll be needing the bigger ones anyway. Instead, purchase bottles

that hold eight to twelve ounces of milk, even if your baby doesn't consume that much in the beginning.

177. Marketers would have you believe that silicone nipples are vastly superior to rubber ones. While they do last longer, it is recommended that nipples be thrown out after six months of use anyway, and rubber will definitely hold up that long.

178. Avoid bottles that come with disposable liners. Your initial investment may not be that much, but they become terribly expensive when you figure the cost of buying liners for a year or more. If your baby is colicky, you should still be able to use regular bottles. As long as you hold them correctly (holding the end of the bottle up all the way to eliminate bubbles), your baby shouldn't get bubbles in her tummy.

179. Another alternative to bottles with liners is the Dr. Brown bottle. It uses a patented system to reduce air bubbles and simulate a natural flow, making it ideal for colicky babies. Dr. Brown bottles are a little bit more expensive than regular bottles, but since they have no disposable parts they are less costly in the long run than using liners.

180. Skip the bottle sterilizer. Running your bottles through the dishwasher should be sufficient to get them clean. If you notice any type of buildup in the bottle or nipple, *FREE* simply boil them in a large pot of water to kill any bacteria.

181. Don't buy those cute little bottles shaped like teddy bears or puppies. Their little nooks and crannies make them extremely hard to clean, and you will most likely end up having to throw them away much sooner than regular bottles.

182. If you're a breast-feeding mom, skip the bottle stage when weaning your child. Most babies can go straight to a spill-proof cup by about six months, saving the expense of bottles. By doing so, you're also avoiding the difficulty some parents experience when taking their child's bottle away.

183. Try a new paintbrush to clean your bottle's nipples. It works just as well as a nipple brush in getting to those hard-to-reach places, and costs much less.

184. When your baby gets a little older, you'll want to get nipples that have larger holes to allow for a faster flow. Enlarge the ones you have already by inserting a toothpick in the nipple and boiling it for a few minutes. Or, insert a sewing needle that has been heated with a match.

185. Don't waste any more money on lost pacifiers. Use Velcro, a suspender clip, and some decorative five-eighths-inch ribbon to make a pacifier clip. Cut the ribbon approximately fourteen to fifteen inches in length. Attach it to the clip on one end, and use the Velcro on the end you'll be threading through the pacifier. You get to customize the look—you can even make several to coordinate with baby's outfits.

186. Generic pacifiers can often be found in packages of two or three at your dollar store. They are similar to the orthodontic latex style, at a fraction of the price.

skip the bottle warmer

187. Skip the bottle warmer. Simply place the bottle in a bowl of warm water for a couple minutes to heat it through. Shake vigorously to make sure it is evenly heated before offering it to your baby.

FREE

188. Your coffee pot works well as a bottle warmer. Use it to keep water warm, then place your bottle in the carafe. Within a couple of minutes, the milk will be heated through.

FREE

189. A slow cooker filled with water and set on low can substitute for a bottle warmer. Just mix the formula and water and place the bottle in the slow cooker. Within a couple of minutes it should be warm enough for your baby.

FREE

190. Remove a bottle filled with formula from the refrigerator right before you go to bed at night. By the time you need it for a late-night feeding, it will be room temperature.

191. For nighttime feedings, boil water in the evening and place it in a thermos. Leave the thermos, formula, and clean bottle on your dresser. When you get up in the middle of the night, you'll be ready to go without having to make a trip to the kitchen.

* chapter 6 *

open wide, baby!

cups and plates

192. Several companies offer disposable spill-proof cups and spoons, which can be found in the infant-feeding section of most large discount stores. Even though they're marketed as disposable, they can be used over and over again. If you lose or damage one, you won't feel bad about having to throw it away.

193. Mold and mildew builds up easily in spill-proof cup lids and stoppers, and their tiny crevices make them very hard to keep clean. Sanitize them easily by soaking them in denture cleaner tablet solution. Use hot water to dilute the tablet and let them soak overnight.

194. Create a nonslip cup by wrapping a few rubber bands around your baby's cup. With a better grip, your baby will be less likely to drop it.

195. A Frisbee turned upside down can be used as a plate for baby.

REUSE

196. Coffee filters or muffin cups double as serving platters for little fingers, and can be tossed when you're through with them. Look for them in bulk at your dollar store.

197. Skip the plate when baby is learning to self-feed. Instead, place food directly on the high chair tray. Babies love to pick up the plate and drop it over the edge of the chair, which creates an even bigger mess than having no plate at all.

198. A cute toddler cup can be made from a honey bottle shaped like a bear. Clean the bottle thoroughly to remove any trace of honey. Then cut the spout off so that you're left with a hole about the diameter of a straw.

REUSE

199. Reuse small plastic baby food containers to carry snacks in your diaper bag or store homemade baby food in the freezer for later use.

REUSE

supermarket baby clubs

200. A&P Baby Bonus Club—http://www.apfreshonline.com/pages_clubCard_BB.asp. Baby Bonus Club members receive a $20 bonus each time their Savings Club purchases add up to $200 in a designated three-month cycle.

201. Food Lion—http://www.foodlion.com/babysteps/0-3/. Visit their site for special offers and printable coupons.

202. Publix Baby Club—http://publix.com/services/clubs/Clubs.do. Publix Baby Club is for parents with kids under the age of two. Benefits include a free newsletter with coupons for free products and various other discounts.

203. Save-a-Lot—http://save-a-lot.com/ ads-promotions/promotions/being-well-baby. Sign up and receive special offers by mail.

204. Shaw's—http://www.shaws.com/ learn/ducklings/index.html. Sign up for in-store promotions, coupons, and special offers.

205. ShopRite Baby Bucks—http://www .shoprite.com/BabyBucks.aspx. Spend $100 on baby items in a three-month cycle and get a $10 coupon with your cash register receipt.

$10

206. Waldbaum's Baby Club—http://www.waldbaums.com/pages_club Card_BB.asp. Members of the Waldbaum's Baby Bonus Savings Club receive a $20 reward each time their Savings Club purchases add up to $200 in a designated three-month cycle.

$20

207. Winn-Dixie Baby Club—http://winn-dixie.com/Better_Rewards/Baby _Club.asp. Get $10 back for every 200 points earned, $10 off baby's first prescription, coupons, and special offers by mail.

$10

208. Redeem your formula checks and other baby coupons at supermarkets that offer baby bucks. In most cases you will get the full value of the item in baby bucks and still receive your coupon discount.

online coupons for baby food

209. Beech-Nut—www.beechnut.com. Click on the "Offers and Partners" tab to see a list of current promotions and coupons. Sign up to receive their free monthly e-newsletters and a new parent packet, which often include valuable coupons to use on Beech-Nut baby foods.

(FREE)

210. Gerber—www.gerber.com. Click on the "Special Offers" tab for contests, coupons, and other promotions.

211. Heinz—www.heinzbaby.com. Click on the "Special Offers" tab to see a list of current promotions and coupons. Sign up to receive their free monthly e-newsletters, which include feeding information and coupons. Their rewards program lets you save UPC points redeemable for baby

toys from companies like Little Tikes. (Some of their programs are limited to Canadian residents only.)

212. Earth's Best—www.earthsbest.com. Click on their "Promotions and Offers" tab for coupons, UPC redemption programs, and links to other special offers.

213. Nature's Goodness—www.natures goodness.com. Join Nature's Goodness Family Club and receive valuable coupons and special offers by mail.

baby food bargains

214. Skip the smallest jars of baby food. Instead, buy the large jars, which are usually more economical and better for the environment. Freeze the excess in ice cube trays. Just pop them out when frozen and store them in a zippered freezer bag.

WORTH IT

215. Before putting those cute little jars in your grocery cart, check to make sure that they haven't passed their expiration date.

216. Be sure to check ingredients in your baby food. While certain brands may be less costly, they may contain more fillers and additives. Therefore, you're having to feed your baby more to get the same amount of nutrition.

WORTH IT

217. Foods marketed to toddlers are a waste of money. They are basically table food cut into smaller, bite-sized pieces. You can create the same thing at home by cutting your own food to accommodate your older baby or toddler.

218. Make candles in glass baby food jars by melting broken crayons and pouring the wax around a length of wick (available at craft stores). Add essential oils in your favorite scent.

REUSE

219. Make a homemade snow globe out of an empty glass baby food jar. Fill the jar with water, leaving one-quarter of an inch at the top. Add a teaspoon of glitter, secure any figurine to the lid with hot glue or polymer clay, and hot glue the lid shut.

REUSE

220. Shop for store-brand, private-label baby food, which almost always costs less than name-brand and is just as good. In some cases, it is even made by the same manufacturer as its name-brand counterpart.

221. Stock up when baby food goes on sale and combine sales with coupons. Just don't buy too much. You won't want baby food on hand when your child outgrows it!

Sixteen Ways to Reuse Glass Baby Food Jars

✳ Store bulk spices or dried herbs from your garden

✳ Store and heat leftovers

✳ Store small barrettes, ponytail holders, or hair clips

✳ Hold water for painting

✳ Store craft supplies

✳ Store nails, screws, and bolts

✳ As a makeup brush, paintbrush, or pen/pencil holder—hot glue several jars together evenly

✳ Use to store jewelry

✳ Use as a cotton swab holder

✳ Store sewing notions, or an emergency sewing kit

✳ Store seeds from your garden for next year

* Fill with homemade gift items such as bath salts, sugar scrubs, flavored oils or vinegars, candy, flavored butters, or tea

* Use to make homemade butter by filling with heavy whipping cream and letting the kids shake it

* Store homemade finger paint

* Keep loose change

* Organize small desk items (paper clips, push-pins, rubber bands)

make it at home

222. Make your own baby food! Cook your vegetables, meat, and fruit, then put them in a blender or food processor and blend well. Spoon the food into ice cube trays to freeze. Empty the ice cubes into freezer bags and thaw them as needed for each serving. Or, plop spoonfuls onto a sheet of wax paper on a cookie sheet and freeze. When you

make your own baby food you can control what goes in it—nothing but food and water, no preservatives or additives. You can also use organic produce.

223. When making your own baby food, freeze a few servings in plastic containers. That way, you can take them out when you're in a hurry or on-the-go. Gerber baby food containers can be used for this and are just the right size.

224. Cream of Wheat is an acceptable substitute for baby cereal. Like baby cereal, it is also fortified with vitamins and iron. It is available in bulk at restaurant/bakery supply stores and warehouse stores like Sam's Club, BJ's, and Costco.

225. Instant oats pulverized in a blender make an instant baby cereal. You can purchase the oats in bulk. Prepare it ahead of time and

store it in an airtight container. When you're ready to use it, just mix it with breast milk, formula, or water.

226. Make your own rice cereal. Start with one-half cup of brown rice, pulverizing it in your blender. Bring two cups of water to a boil. Reduce the heat and add the rice. Stir briskly, and remove it from the burner. Cover and let it stand for ten minutes, stirring occasionally to prevent sticking and clumping.

227. If you're breast-feeding, waiting a little longer to start your baby on solid food can help you save money. Most pediatricians recommend starting solids between ages four and six months. By putting off starting solids until your baby is closer to six months, you are saving money on baby food. Besides, your baby is getting all the nutrition he needs in your milk.

228. When your baby starts to eat table food, puree or chop up your leftovers, put them in baby food jars, and freeze them. Be sure to mark the date on the jar. If you add a lot of seasoning to your foods, be sure to make baby's serving first and leave the spices out.

229. Make the switch to table food early rather than relying on jarred baby food. Gradually add more and more texture to your baby's diet, so that by seven or eight months your baby will be able to eat bite-sized pieces of avocado, peas, cooked carrots, and so forth. He will also have lots of fun feeding himself!

230. Peel a ripe banana and spoon-feed it to baby. This costs much less than a jar of baby food, and is virtually the same thing!

231. Buy cottage cheese (large-curd works best) and rinse it in a colander. The pieces that remain are great for self-feeders.

232. Other great foods for babies ready to self-feed include ripe bananas (cut into small pieces), cooked carrots, Cheerios, egg yolks (skip the whites before baby is one year old), green beans, graham crackers, noodles, pears, peas, sweet potatoes, squash, rice, and rice cakes. Remember to cook vegetables thoroughly so they're soft.

233. Prepare cereal with very little liquid so that it has a thick, clumpy consistency. Babies who are learning to self-feed can use their fingers to pick it up.

234. If you don't have enough time to make your own baby food, buy foods marketed to adults that work for baby. Unsweetened applesauce, for example, works well for baby because it is the same consistency as baby food.

235. No matter how cheap it may be priced, it's never safe to feed your baby these foods: peanuts and other nuts, popcorn, hot dogs, sausages, grapes, apple chunks, raw carrots, peanut butter, and other hard meats.

236. You can often save quite a bit by buying baby food by the case at warehouse stores like Sam's Club, Costco, and BJ's Discount Club. Even superstores like Babies "R" Us and Toys "R" Us stock baby food.

237. When buying cases of baby food, you can use more than one coupon. For example, if you have a coupon for $0.50 off eight jars, you can use three coupons on a case of twenty-four jars.

238. Don't buy juices for your baby in the baby food aisle. Instead, make your own using 100 percent fruit juice and adding water. Juices for babies are really just regular juice with a higher water concentration and a little vitamin C added. Your baby should be getting a sufficient supply of vitamin C in breast milk or formula already. Mix about one-half water to one-half juice. Avoid juices like orange juice, which may upset little tummies, and apple cider that is unpasteurized.

239. If your baby is partial to that thick, smooth, congealed texture that baby food is famous for, add a little bit of boiled potato to his food when you puree it.

240. Buy snacks such as graham crackers, Cheerios, and animal crackers in bulk. Break down the bag to smaller bags and freeze them to keep them fresh.

241. Make your own Zwieback teething biscuits. Simply cut pieces of bread into strips or squares, and bake it in the oven at a very low temperature (150 to 200 degrees) for fifteen to twenty minutes. Dark, dense breads such as wheat and rye work best.

242. A frozen bagel works well as a teether for your baby. The cold feels great on her gums, and the bagel is easy to hold. While baby can gnaw on it quite a while without making any progress, be careful that she doesn't get any bites that are big enough for her to choke on.

fancy bibs get dirty, too

243. Make your own bib by taking a cloth napkin or kitchen towel and securing it behind baby's neck with a safety pin (the kind used with cloth diapers) or a mitten clip. Keep a safety pin in your diaper bag for this purpose, in case you forget to pack a bib.

244. An old bandana or scarf tied behind baby's neck also doubles as a bib. A man's handkerchief can be used for this purpose as well.

245. Don't bother with fancy burp cloths. Get a pack of old-fashioned cloth diapers—great for burping and spitting up, and also great as rags when you are done with them! Or simply use a dishtowel.

REUSE

246. A plastic grocery bag can be made into a disposable bib by slitting the back and bottom. Use the handles as sleeves. Throw a couple bags into your diaper bag to have ready for eating out.

247. Another great bib can be made from a dishtowel. Cut a hole for the neck in the back third of the towel, and sew on some ribbing (or the neckline of an old T-shirt). These bibs slide easily over a baby's head and are big enough to provide complete coverage.

248. You can make your own baby bibs inexpensively by purchasing kids' T-shirts or sweatshirts secondhand. Leaving the front and its design, cut off the sleeves and the back. Finish the edges using a zigzag stitch or with a serger.

baby's

health and

hygiene

* chapter 7 *

diapering your
new bundle

disposable diapers

249. Buy diapers in bulk. As a general rule, the larger the package the lower the price per unit. Those big boxes may be harder to lug home, but they'll end up saving you money.

250. If you're using coupons to buy diapers, however, it is best to get the smallest size package available. For example, $2 off a

$10 package yields a higher percentage savings than $2 off a $20 package.

251.

Store-brand diapers from Target and Wal-Mart are just as absorbent as premium diapers and cost about $0.10 per diaper less. The savings can add up to as much as $30 per month.

$30/MONTH

252.

Visit the Huggies website for printable coupons and information on special offers and promotions: www.huggies.com.

253.

Luvs brand diapers cost 20 percent less than other premium diapers, and offer coupons as well, which can sometimes bring their cost below store brands. Visit their website to sign up for promotions: www.luvsdiapers.com.

20% OFF

254. Check warehouse stores like Costco, BJ's, and Sam's Club for diapers. Most offer cases of premium diaper brands at a substantial discount. Don't forget to bring your coupons along when you head to BJ's for even more savings. They're currently the only warehouse store that accepts them.

255. Check Amazon.com for diapers. They frequently run sales on Pampers, Huggies, and Seventh Generation and offer free shipping if you spend a certain amount. No lugging those big boxes home—they'll ship them direct to your door!

256. Combining manufacturer's coupons and in-store sales can bring the cost of premium diapers to less than that of store brands, especially if your local grocer doubles coupons.

257. Buy the smallest size diaper your baby can fit into comfortably. While diaper packs cost the same, the larger sizes have fewer diapers inside each package. Therefore, larger diapers of the same brand are more costly.

258. If the diaper brand you are using is leaking, it can be a sign that you need to go up a size rather than to switch to a more expensive brand.

259. If you find a diaper that is missing tabs or defective in some way, contact the manufacturer. They will likely send coupons, sometimes even for free products.

260. If your child has a tendency to soak through his diaper overnight, try placing a maxi pad inside the diaper rather than

double-diapering him. Another solution is to use inexpensive diapers during the day and premium diapers at night.

261. Visit the Seventh Generation website for coupons good for their bleach-and chlorine-free baby diapers when you sign up for their free Seventh Generation Nation club: http://www.seventhgeneration.com/coupons.

262. Visit the Goodnites website and find coupons in their "Special Offers" section: www.goodnites.com.

263. Register for Pampers' Gifts to Grow program and you will receive samples and coupons for Pampers products. You'll also be able to enter the codes from the products you buy to earn rewards such as toys and gift cards: www.pampers.com.

264. Don't stock up on diapers if your baby is nearing the next size. You don't want to be stuck with a half-used package.

265. Diapers can occasionally be found at thrift stores like Goodwill and the Salvation Army. Stores often donate packs that have been opened or damaged in some way. Parents will donate partial packs when their kids outgrow a certain size.

266. Use the big boxes/cartons that diapers come in to store outgrown baby clothes. The boxes are already marked according-ing to size, so you'll know what size the clothes are.

REUSE

267. Coupons for diapers and wipes can also be found on eBay. Search for

keywords according to your favorite brand. Make sure you check the seller's feedback rating and find out what the expiration dates are before placing your bid.

268. If you do use premium diaper brands, ask your friends and family to cut coupons for you. Most are happy to help you out and don't mind taking the time to do so.

269. Join an online coupon trading community to trade diaper coupons with other moms. Mommysavers.com has a bartering board where you can post your requests: www .mommysavers.com.

270. The swim diapers that parents use for small children when swimming in the pool are very expensive (most are around $0.75 per diaper). Most people don't realize that

they can be machine-washed and used again. Just make sure you air-dry them and do not put them in the dryer.

271. Look for swim diaper coupons on-line. Check the Little Swimmers website and click on their "Special Offers" tab: http://www.littleswimmers.com/na/offers/offers.asp.

cloth diapers

272. There's no reason not to try cloth diapers if you have time to launder them. Cloth diapers are better and easier to use than ever. Now they even come with Velcro closures and can be used with disposable liners. Using cloth vs. disposable diapers can save your family up to $25 per month.

273. Start small. Buy about half the cloth diapers you think you'll need and commit to using them part-time in the beginning. You can always increase your usage if you decide to do so.

274. Skip the newborn size with cloth diapers. Because your baby will outgrow them so quickly, it is usually cheaper to use disposables during this stage. Plus, cloth diapering does require a time commitment. When your baby is a newborn, you will need the extra time to rest.

275. While they save money in the long run, cloth diapers cost more with the initial investment. Contact diaper manufacturers to see if they would provide you with a trial pack or diaper sample to allow you to try them before making your investment.

276. If you're hesitant about giving cloth diapering a try because you don't want to be swamped with laundry, consider a diaper service. Most large cities have them. Using a service still may be more economical than using disposables, especially if you have more than one child in diapers.

277. Ask a diaper service what they do with their "retired" diapers. Most dispose of them or will sell them at rock-bottom prices. In most cases, they still have a lot of wear left!

278. When selecting your diapers, make sure to choose diaper-service-quality prefolds. This type has thick padding in the middle (Chinese prefolds are considered the best). Diapers from discount stores are less expensive, but are much less absorbent.

WORTH IT

279. If you're using prefolded diapers, they should be absorbent enough so that you don't need liners. If you're anticipating a leak, you can use an inexpensive thinner cloth diaper folded inside the prefolded one as a liner.

280. Shop for cloth diapers online. EBay also has a steady supply of new and gently used cloth diapers for sale.

281. Post a request for gently used cloth diapers on a bartering board. In all likelihood there's a mom out there who has just potty-trained her child and is looking to give the diapers a new home. Check out Mommysavers.com's Bartering Board: www.mommysavers.com.

282. Diaper liners that haven't gotten too messy can be washed and reused several times. When they get dirty, just throw them away. A box of fifty liners can last several months!

REUSE

283. Cut your cost even more when cloth diapering by making your own diapers. You can find patterns online, or you can even make your own pattern by tracing a diaper you already have. The materials required are very inexpensive. Some people even make diapers by recycling old receiving blankets or flannel sheets!

284. It's not all-or-nothing. Even using cloth diapers while you're home can save money. Working moms can use cloth at home and send disposables with baby to day care.

285. Instead of buying disposable swim diapers, buy a fabric one that can be machine-washed. One fabric swim diaper costs about the same as a pack of disposables, but can be used over and over again.

> ### Seven Ways to Reuse Cloth Diapers
>
> * Dusting rags
>
> * Washing the car
>
> * Shop rags
>
> * Polishing silver
>
> * Reusable cotton pads (instead of cotton balls)
>
> * Mopping the floor
>
> * Make a hot pad

286. Reuse extra diaper pins to pin dirty socks together before tossing in the washing machine. Since there's no sock sorting after doing laundry, it's a huge time-saver. Plus, *(REUSE)* you'll avoid those "missing sock" mysteries.

washing cloth diapers

287. When laundering diapers, first run them through a cold rinse cycle adding half a cup of baking soda to the water. This will whiten your diapers, remove odors, and neutralize acidity levels.

288. Fabric softener should not be used when laundering cloth diapers. It causes a waxy buildup on the diapers, reducing the absorbency and making the diapers water-repellent.

289. Vinegar is a natural fabric softener that removes all traces of detergent and ammonia (urine smell) from the diapers, lowers the pH level (which helps to prevent diaper rashes), and helps to whiten the diapers. Add a Downy ball half full of white vinegar. It will open up in the final rinse cycle, and soften them.

290. Bleach can damage the fibers of your cloth diapers, so use it sparingly. Use chlorine-free bleach or borax instead.

291. Try drying your stained diapers on the clothesline in the sun to bleach the stains. The sun will whiten them, and the fresh air will make them smell great!

FREE

292. Certain diaper rash ointments can leave gray stains on your diapers. Use a cream that does not contain any cod-liver (fish) oils and you'll avoid such stains.

baby wipes

293. In most cases, store-brand wipes are just as good as premium wipes. Be sure to give the ones from Target and Wal-Mart a try. Mothers also rave about wipes from discount warehouse Costco.

294. Thick premium baby wipes can be machine-washed and reused. Soak them in the baby wipe solution mentioned in tip #298 and store them in the original baby wipes container.

295. Cut or tear commercial diaper wipes in half. That way, you're not using more than you actually need.

296. If you use commercial baby wipes, buy refill packs instead of purchasing a new container each time. You can buy refills of premium and store-brand wipes in bulk at warehouse clubs like Sam's Club, BJ's, and Costco.

297. Make your own baby wipes at home. It's quick and easy, and these wipes are a fraction of the cost of premium wipes. For instructions, see the following page.

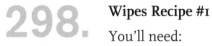

298. Wipes Recipe #1

You'll need:

1 roll of premium-brand paper towels (Bounty or Viva work well)

2-1/4 cups water

2 tablespoons baby bath or shampoo

1 tablespoon of baby oil

Cut the roll of paper towels in half using an electric knife. Mix all the liquid ingredients together. Put towels in a round plastic container and pour the liquid over the top. Let the mixture soak through for five to ten minutes and pull out the center core. Wipes will pop up through the middle. *Note: Don't try to save money by using a cheap brand of paper towels. The towels will disintegrate.

299. **Wipes Recipe #2**
Instead of soaking the paper towels in a solution, keep the solution in a spray bottle and spray the paper towel or a baby washcloth when ready to use.

300. Instead of disposable baby wipes, consider using lightweight baby washcloths to wipe your baby. Not only are they reusable, you can wipe your baby with a warm washcloth instead of a cold one.

REUSE

301. Some of the softest baby wipes can be made from old receiving blankets. Simply cut them into rectangles and serge the edges with a sewing machine to keep them from fraying.

302. Skip the wipe warmer. They only hold a small amount of wipes, and by the time the wipe reaches your baby's bottom it may not even be that warm anymore. Plus, many older models have been recalled due to overheating. They can also dry out your wipes.

303. Just hold a wipe in your hand for a minute to take the chill off. Body heat is free!

FREE

304. Store your container of baby wipes upside down. This helps to ensure that the top wipe will be equally as moist as the bottom one.

305. If your wipes get dried out, don't throw them away. Simply add a little water and let it soak through.

REUSE

306. Don't buy individual small packages of wipes for travel. Instead, put some wipes or even a wet washcloth in a ziplock bag. When you're done, you can use the bag for diaper disposal as well.

Eight Ways to Reuse Baby Wipe Containers

✳ Store homemade wipes (see pages 124 and 125 for instructions)

✳ Store small toys, puzzle pieces, or playing cards

✳ Store ribbon or other craft supplies

✳ Store accessories such as socks, hairbows, or tights

✳ Use to store nail polish, emery boards, and fingernail clippers

✳ Organize baby's bottle or sippy cup pieces (valves, nipples, lids)

* Use for under-sink storage (sponges, stoppers, scrubbers) in the kitchen.

* Store plastic bags.

307. If you use washcloths for wiping baby, use the color-coding system. For example, use one color of washcloths for diaper wipes and another color for bathing baby.

308. Other uses for baby wipes include cleaning leather, cleaning baby's car seat, spot-cleaning carpet and upholstery, and removing deodorant and lipstick from clothing.

309. Skip the wipes altogether. Use a hand-shower in the bath when baby has an especially messy diaper—the kind that really sticks to the bottom. Instead of wasting five to ten wipes trying to get the mess off, just place your baby in the tub. A handheld shower works really well to get it off his tiny bottom, and is much less irritating to his skin.

diaper covers

310. While diaper covers are helpful, it isn't necessary to use them all the time. If you're using a high-quality diaper and change it frequently, you should be able to get by without them. Just purchase a couple in the beginning for overnights, long car rides, and other situations where leaks may occur.

311. Choose a breathable fabric instead of plastic for diaper covers. Because they don't allow air to circulate, plastic diaper covers tend to keep too much moisture near baby's skin. The added moisture often leads to diaper rash. Choose diaper covers in nylon or another breathable fabric for baby to wear over her diaper to prevent leaks when needed. While nylon diaper covers are more expensive than plastic, they do last longer.

WORTH IT

diaper pails

312. The plastic bags in which newspapers are delivered are great for wrapping and disposing of dirty diapers. Bread bags and plastic grocery bags also work well.

REUSE

313. Consider using a regular trash can, preferably the kind with the step-on lid opener, for disposing of baby's diapers. Place them in a plastic bag first. Sprinkle a little cat litter *REUSE* in the bottom of the can to absorb the odor.

314. Most dollar stores carry diaper disposal bags in boxes of one hundred for a dollar. They are great for use at home, or to pack away in your diaper bag.

315. Reuse bags from diapers and wipe refills to hold a dirty diaper. *REUSE* Use a twist tie if there isn't a zip closure.

316. If you buy a Diaper Genie, factor in the cost of the refills. Diaper Genie diaper disposal systems run about $25 if purchased new. However, most moms don't factor in the price

of refills when they buy one. At $6 to $7 a refill, these systems can be quite costly over time. Some parents use them for dirty diapers only, throwing the wet ones in the regular trash, which also saves quite a bit on refills.

317. An alternative to the best-selling Diaper Genie is the Diaper Champ by Baby Trend. While the initial investment is about the same, the Diaper Champ uses regular garbage bags as opposed to the expensive refills its competitor requires.

318. Most diaper pails are $25 if purchased new. They can often be found for $5 or less at thrift stores and garage sales, and with a little bleach and warm water, they are as good as new!

80% OFF

319. If you do use the Diaper Genie, look for partially used refills at thrift stores or garage sales. Sometimes you can find a used Diaper Genie with the refill left inside for $5 or less. The extra Diaper Genie can be used in another room, or at Grandma's house.

diaper rash

320. If your baby has diaper rash, have him sit in a bath with a little baking soda added. It clears up mild rashes quickly!

321. Keep the diaper off your baby for fifteen to thirty minutes after changing him. This will allow air to circulate and promote healing.

FREE

322. Check your wipes. Commercial baby wipes containing alcohol will irritate your baby's skin and make diaper rash worse. Discontinue use until the rash has cleared up, using a warm washcloth instead.

323. Petroleum jelly is a great preventative measure to use if your baby is prone to diaper rash. Apply a thin coat after each diaper change, and you'll notice fewer breakouts. It also makes wiping a messy bottom much easier.

324. An even cheaper alternative to petroleum jelly is vegetable shortening. Use it just as you would any diaper rash cream, applying a thin coat with every diaper change to act as a barrier against wetness.

325. Another way to clear up diaper rash is to wash your baby's bottom and dry it with a hairdryer. Make sure your dryer is set on the coolest setting possible, and keep it a safe distance from baby's bottom (at least six inches away).

FREE

326. In the summer, look for plain zinc oxide to use in preventing and treating diaper rash. Zinc oxide is the active ingredient in most commercial diaper rash creams, and is marketed as a sunscreen. It's usually a lot cheaper and just as effective.

327. Many moms swear by the antacid method. Apply a little liquid antacid such as Maalox or Mylanta with a cotton ball to baby's bottom. It will soothe baby's skin and neutralize acid.

328. Try an antifungal cream. Creams like those used to treat athlete's foot, such as Lotrimin AF, are also known to clear up diaper rash.

329. Less is more when it comes to diaper rash ointment and creams. Slathering on too much does more harm than good. Apply a thin coat, allowing your baby's skin to breathe.

330. Skip the baby powder. Most parents believe that sprinkling a little baby powder on baby's skin after a diaper change will absorb any extra moisture. All it really does is clump up when it gets damp, holding the moisture next to your baby's skin. It also poses a health risk to babies who accidentally inhale it. It's best not to use anything at all.

331. Rather than spending money on disposable changing pads, make your own out of a vinyl tablecloth. They can be cut into generous-sized rectangles and folded to fit in your diaper bag. They are still inexpensive enough to throw away when they get really messy.

* chapter 8 *
baby in the bath

saving money at bath time

332. A large Rubbermaid container can double as a baby bath. Plus, when you're done using it as a tub, it works great to store outgrown baby clothing.

REUSE

333. A baby bathtub can almost always be found at a thrift store or garage sale for a couple of dollars, much less than the $20 to $35 it costs in retail stores. Your infant will only need it for a couple of months before graduating to the big tub.

80% OFF

334. Baby bathtubs with a mesh cover or cradle cost more than the standard models. By slipping a pillowcase over a standard tub, you create the same thing.

335. Consider buying an inflatable tub for your baby. It costs less than a regular baby tub and can be deflated and packed in your suitcase for travel. It also makes a fun outdoor pool for your baby in the summertime.

WORTH IT

336. Skip the baby bathtub altogether. Instead, bathe your baby in the kitchen sink. The sink is at a better level for a parent to bathe a child comfortably, and the spray nozzle is a nice feature to have when rinsing. Use a rubber sink mat to prevent slipping.

337. Consider giving your baby a bath while you take yours. Just make sure that the water isn't too hot. An elbow in the tub is a more reliable check than using your hand.

338. Instead of buying a nonskid liner or baby bumpers for your bathtub (which can run well over $20), place a towel on the bottom of the tub to prevent your child from sliding around.

FREE

339. Don't buy those thin towels for baby. The towels the rest of your family uses are just fine, and much more absorbent. Look for towels to go on sale during the year, or during traditional January white sales.

340. Set your hot water heater no higher than 120 degrees to avoid scalding your baby. Plus, you'll save money on your heating bill by keeping the setting low.

341. A hooded towel can be made inexpensively at home by sewing a washcloth and towel together. Fold the washcloth in half so that it looks like a rectangle. Sew one short end closed, open out the other short end of the washcloth, center it on the long side of the bath towel, and stitch it together. The homemade version is much warmer and more absorbent than the flimsy ones marketed

for infants. Plus, as the child grows the towel serves as a great swimming cover-up.

342. When you're done using your receiving blankets, cut them into squares to use as washcloths for baby.

(REUSE)

343. It isn't necessary to give your baby a bath more than once or twice a week. Frequent bathing not only wastes baby wash, it often leads to dry skin.

344. Don't buy a bath seat or ring designed to keep your child upright while sitting in the tub. Most have suction cups that can come unstuck, causing your baby to topple over and become pinned under the water.

345. Don't purchase a bath visor to keep water and soap out of baby's eyes. Instead, swipe a little petroleum jelly in a line on his forehead. It will deflect the water away from his face.

346. When your baby is making the transition from a baby bathtub to the big tub, use a plastic laundry basket if he is able to sit in it upright. Store bath toys in the basket when it's not in use.

REUSE

toiletries

347. Baby bath soaps aren't necessary. Using a mild, gentle bar soap such as Dove, Aveeno, or Neutrogena works just as well and is much less expensive.

348. Call Boudreaux's Butt Paste at 1-800-252-4739 to receive free samples of many of their products.

(FREE)

349. The dollar store can be a great place to pick up toiletries such as shampoos, lotions, and washcloths for your baby. Sometimes they even carry name brands.

350. Make your own hair detangler by combining one part conditioner with ten parts water. Mix well and pour into a spray pump, using a funnel to avoid spilling.

351. If you use bar soap for baby, put it in an old sock to make it easier to hold.

352. Visit the Playtex website and sign up for their newsletter. (Playtex manufactures Diaper Genie, Baby Magic, bottles, cups, etc.) You'll get the scoop on new products, free samples, and special offers: www.playtexbaby.com.

353. It isn't necessary to buy both baby shampoo and baby wash. Instead, opt for just the baby wash, which doubles as both a soap and a shampoo.

354. Contact Johnson & Johnson at 1-800-526-3967 or visit their website, www.johnsonsbaby.com, for free product coupons and information on bathing your baby.

355. Buy generic or store-brand baby wash and shampoo. There is little or no difference between the cheaper versions and the more expensive name brands. Plus, they smell just as good!

356. Contact Baby Orajel for information on teeth and gum care for infants. When you sign up, you may receive coupons and samples in the mail: www.orajel.com.

357. Avoid buying toiletries at the grocery store, where the markup is high. Instead, look for them at pharmacies like CVS, Walgreen's, and Rite Aid where you can combine in-store sales with coupons and rebate programs.

358. Extend your baby wash by using a suds pump. Fill the pump one-third of the way with baby wash, then fill to just an inch below the top with water. Pampered Chef makes a great one that sells for around $11.50, or simply refill an old one.

359. Unless you live in a particularly dry climate, you probably won't use very much baby lotion. The lotion the rest of the family uses is fine for baby.

bath toys

360. Skip the fancy bath toy holder. Instead, opt for a plain mesh laundry bag (if the bag is too large, simply tie a knot in the bottom). The mesh allows the water to drain, preventing any mold or mildew from forming on your baby's toys. Look for one at your dollar store.

361. There's no need to spend money on expensive bath toys for baby. Plastic lids and containers are great for tub time, as well as toys your baby probably already has like stacking cups, plastic key rings, and teethers. Other great toys include turkey basters, Styrofoam trays, colanders, and sponges.

REUSE

362. Keep your baby's bath toys clean by throwing them in the washing machine with your shower curtain. Add a little bleach to kill any mildew or bacteria.

363. The mesh bag that oranges come in also works well for bath toy storage. Hang from the faucet or showerhead to maximize drainage.

REUSE

364. Use a large plastic planter to store your baby's tub toys. It has holes in the bottom for drainage, and a tray to collect excess water. Plus, you can use it to plant flowers when you're done using it for baby.

(REUSE)

fun stuff

365. Make your own bath paints. Add a little food coloring to liquid hand soap, and place the soap in disposable plastic containers.

366. Fill your ice cube trays with water, adding a drop of food coloring to each section. When frozen, these can be popped out and placed in baby's bathwater. He'll have fun "chasing" them around in the tub and trying to grab for them before they melt.

367. Save your baby's tub when he's outgrown it. It can double as a mini-sandbox or a place to store bath toys.

REUSE

368. Bathtub soap crayons can be made by mixing half a cup of soap flakes (grating a bar of Ivory works well), one to two tablespoons of hot water, and a little food coloring. Place the mixture in molds like ice cube trays or muffin tins until dry (this can take up to a week).

369. Make your own homemade bath time finger paint by combining shaving cream, food coloring, and a couple of tablespoons of dish soap. Your child will have lots of fun "painting" the tub with this concoction!

370. Create your own bubble bath by mixing a little liquid dish soap under the running water. Don't use too much, as the detergent can be harsh on baby's skin.

cutting baby's hair

371. Cutting baby's hair can be almost as expensive as getting your own hair cut. It's hard to find a stylist that doesn't charge at least $10 for a simple trim. Instead, invest in a pair of hair-cutting scissors and learn how to trim your child's hair at home. Instructional videos can be found on YouTube to make it even easier.

WORTH IT

372. A sun visor can be helpful when cutting your child's bangs. Lay the hair over the visor, and then cut. Your child is less likely to feel anything while you're cutting, and you end up with a straighter line.

373. For cutting bangs, place a piece of Scotch tape right at the level you want to cut. Cut just above the line, and the tape comes off with the hair. You'll have less mess and a straighter line.

374. A vacuum hair-cutting system can be used to trim hair of various lengths. It uses the suction power of your vacuum, leaving no mess. They can be found for less than $50 on eBay by searching names like "Flowbee" and "RoboCut."

chapter 9

under-the-weather baby

tips for a sick baby

375. Make a soothing bath for baby with oatmeal. Put plain oatmeal in the blender and pulse until powdery. Add about one half cup in the tub water for a soothing oatmeal bath. This works well for diaper rash, too.

376. To avoid wasting medicine, put the required dosage in a bottle nipple and push it through the hole with a clean finger. Baby won't realize it's not milk until he's taken the full dose. Or, ask your pharmacist for a free infant syringe.

377. Visit the American Academy of Pediatrics website for information related to pediatric issues and conditions. The site includes articles written by leading health experts and recommendations supported with scientific research: www.aap.org.

378. Buy store-brand or generic whenever possible when buying over-the-counter medications for baby (or filling a prescription). They typically cost 50 percent less and are just as effective. Often they are even produced by the same manufacturer, just given a different label.

379. An aloe plant is good to have around. Cut the leaves and use the aloe to treat bites, stings, or any other ailment.

380. Under the Vaccines for Children program, low-income families can receive free or low-cost immunizations for their children. Every child up to eighteen years of age who is enrolled in Medicaid, who lacks health insurance, or whose health insurance does not cover vaccines is eligible. For more information, visit the Centers for Disease Control website: www.cdc.gov.

381. If your doctor writes your child a prescription, ask if he or she has any samples of the medication to give you. It may save you a trip to the pharmacist and an expensive co-pay.

FREE

382. Put your family's toothbrushes in the dishwasher every few days to sanitize them, preventing the spread of germs.

congestion

383. For colds and congestion, have your baby sit in the bathroom while you run a hot shower. The warm, moist air helps loosen any phlegm.

384. Onion makes an inexpensive natural decongestant for your baby. Cut an onion into chunks and place them in a bowl. Sprinkle them with a tablespoon of sugar, cover, and refrigerate them for a couple of hours. The syrup that is created makes a great natural decongestant, and is sweet to the taste.

385. A vaporizer is effective in treating congested babies. Choose a cool-mist over a hot-steam humidifier. The hot steam poses a risk of burns or scalding. Look for a used one and sanitize it by washing it with hot water and vinegar or a little bleach.

386. To alleviate sleep problems while your child is congested, have her sleep in her infant car seat or put a phone book or pillow under one end of the crib. Breathing is easier with the head slightly elevated.

constipation

387. Adding a little bit of prune juice to baby's bottle can help if he's constipated. Start by adding just a couple of teaspoons to the bottle and filling the bottle with milk.

stomach illnesses and colic

388. For gassy tummies, put a few ounces of warm water in a bottle. Add a pinch of sugar, and mix it thoroughly. Give the sweetened water to baby and burp her well.

389. Follow the "ABC" method for treating diarrhea. Apples, bananas, and cereal all help. If your child isn't old enough for solid foods, try adding a little rice water (the water rice is cooked in) to her formula.

390. Avoid giving your baby juice if he has diarrhea. It can be too acidic and will often further aggravate the problem.

391. Preserve linens by placing a beach towel on your baby's bedding when he's sick. A towel is easier to remove in the middle of the night than changing a sheet.

392. If your child vomits on the floor, sprinkle a little cat litter over it to absorb the wetness and the smell. Sweep up after a couple minutes. Baking soda also works well.

393. Make your own electrolyte solution at home by combining:

2 quarts water

1 teaspoon salt

1 teaspoon baking soda

1/2 cup sugar

1 packet Kool-Aid

394. Gatorade diluted with 50 percent water is also effective in rehydrating baby and much less expensive than over-the-counter electrolyte solutions.

395. Any baby showing signs of dehydration should be under the care of a physician. Symptoms include crying with no tears, decreased urination (less than four wet diapers in twenty-four hours), dry mouth and tongue, sunken eyes, grayish skin, and a sunken fontanel (soft spot) on baby's head. Do not attempt to treat these symptoms at home.

396. For colicky, crampy babies, put half a peppermint candy in a bottle of warm water. When it has dissolved a little, shake the bottle until the water turns pink and remove the remaining candy. The peppermint is sweet-tasting and acts as an anti-gas agent. It costs much less than expensive anti-gas drops and is just as effective.

397. Gripe Water, which can be found at your pharmacy for about $10, is a tried-and-true colic remedy.

398. Avoid broccoli, asparagus, cabbage, and other gassy foods while breast-feeding. Wheat and dairy can also trigger colic in your baby. Try eating a bland diet for a while, adding more and more foods gradually so that trigger foods can be easily identified.

399. Gentle pressure applied to baby's tummy can help ease the discomfort of colic. Lay your baby facedown over your knees while you rub his back.

400. The SleepTight Infant Soother is a device that attaches to your baby's crib and generates white noise similar to that of a

moving car and claims to effectively reduce colic and crying. Because the SleepTight Infant Soother has been classified by the U.S. Food and Drug Administration as a medical device it may be covered by your health insurance. Visit their website for more information: www.colic.com.

401. Other inexpensive ways to lull colicky babies to sleep include rocking, swinging, bouncing, swaddling, taking him for a ride in the car, or white noise.

teething

402. When your baby starts getting teeth, an alternative to a teething ring is a clean, damp washcloth. Babies love to chew on them, and the cool wet water feels good on their gums. You can even soak it in a little bit of apple juice and put it in the freezer.

FREE

403. Other teething remedies include: a bottle of cold water, hard teething biscuits, frozen bananas, ice chips, cold apple wedges, and cold carrot sticks. Use these methods with close parental supervision to make sure bits and pieces don't come off and become lodged in baby's throat.

404. Simply rubbing or massaging your baby's gums is effective in treating the pain associated with teething.

FREE

405. Over-the-counter teething gels aren't all that effective in alleviating pain. They are topical anesthetics that numb the surface of the gums, but don't do much about the pain underneath. Acetaminophen or other infant pain relievers are more effective in reducing the pain and are more long-lasting.

skin conditions

406. Cradle cap is a common ailment in newborns that can be remedied easily for just pennies. Use a pea-sized amount of any dandruff shampoo on your baby's scalp and brush gently with a toothbrush. The flakes should come right off.

407. Another method for removing cradle cap is to rub a little olive or vegetable oil onto your baby's scalp and gently rub it.

408. If your baby develops baby acne, a few drops of breast milk rubbed onto her skin may help clear it up. Breast milk contains antibacterial properties that can also help heal scratches (from baby's long fingernails) much more *FREE* quickly than without it.

spending time in the sun

409. For a natural sunscreen, choose a mineral sunscreen like zinc oxide and titanium-dioxide-based products rather than chemical-based sunscreens. Look for ones with organic, natural oil bases such as olive, coconut, or shea butter.

410. You don't have to buy sunscreen marketed for babies. Frequently the only difference between adult and baby sunscreen is the fragrance. Make sure you look for one that blocks both UVA and UVB rays.

411. Use clothing to shield baby from the sun. Lightweight cotton fabric and floppy hats are great choices.

412. A sunscreen stick or sunscreen wipes are a good investment. Often it is hard to get sunscreen on baby's face without it dripping and irritating her eyes.

(WORTH IT)

413. Sunscreen expires. Check the date, or call the manufacturer and give them the code on the bottle to see if yours is still effective.

414. Buy store-brand or generic sunscreen if possible. It is just as effective in blocking harmful rays as the name-brand counterparts and costs much less.

other situations

415. Breast milk and its healing properties can be used to help children with pink eye. Just a few drops in the eye will help speed healing.

(FREE)

416. Putting a couple of drops of rubbing alcohol in your child's ear after swimming can help prevent swimmer's ear.

417. Small packages of ketchup, mustard, etc., can be placed in the freezer to be used as ice packs for small cuts, scrapes, or abrasions.

(REUSE)

418. Make your own heating pad for baby by sewing two squares of fabric together and filling it with rice. Put the heating pad in the microwave until it is warm. It can also be used as a trivet or a stress-relieving pillow for mom.

getting

baby
dressed

bargains on baby clothes

used clothing

419. If you're apprehensive about buying used clothing, don't be. Washing it in hot water will get rid of any dirt and germs. Look in your closet. It's *all* used clothing now, whether or not it was purchased that way.

420. Write a "shopping list" before you set out to buy used clothing. It's tempting to overbuy when prices are so low, but having too many clothes can add to the clutter in your dressers and closets making it hard to stay organized. Instead, try to stick to what you need.

421. If you need to buy several things, consider looking for groups of clothing called "lots" on eBay or Craigslist. You'll avoid having to pay multiple shipping charges by buying all you need in one auction and/or shipment, plus you'll pay less per piece overall.

422. Some of the best deals on gently used clothing are outfits for special occasions, dress shoes, and Halloween costumes. Chances are they've been worn very few times and are still in good condition.

423. If you receive hand-me-downs from a friend or relative, be sure to send a thank-you note. It will make the giver feel great about giving you the clothing and make them more likely to want to do it again. Then, be sure you pay it forward when the opportunity arises!

424. Garage sales are a *must* for thrifty parents. This is where you can find used clothing at 75 percent to 90 percent off the retail price. Because infants outgrow clothes so quickly, there is very minimal wear and tear. You can get some beautiful quality name-brand clothes for a steal. (See pages 210–216 for more garage sale shopping tips.)

90% OFF

425. Consignment or resale stores are typically the most expensive places to buy used clothing. Most items are priced about a third or half of what you'd pay for new items. However, they also offer a much wider selection than garage sales or

thrift stores. They are also good when you're looking for something specific: a blue shirt to match a certain sweater, a specific type of shoe, etc.

426. Organize a clothing exchange with friends and/or family. Ask participants to save the clothes that their children grow out of, or do not want anymore. You can then go through the clothes and see what you want to keep.

FREE

427. When babies begin to crawl, they can be really tough on the knees of their pants. Buy iron-on knee enforcement patches for them. Instead of patching them on the outside, iron them on the *inside* of the pants. You will get the same benefit and your baby's clothes will look much better.

428. When your baby outgrows her clothes, swap them for something you can use. Sites like www.swapbabygoods.com help make it easier to trade with other parents who may be looking for what you no longer need. Regular listings are free.

FREE

new clothing

429. Most moms have a tendency to overbuy their kids' clothes. They see something cute at a good price and just can't resist. It isn't a bargain if you don't need it! Not only will this help your budget, you'll gain valuable closet space too.

430. Soak new dark-colored clothing in a solution of cold water and half a cup of vinegar before washing for the first time. This will set the colors and prevent fading.

431. If you're concerned about pilling, try to avoid clothing with polyester. One hundred percent cotton clothing is more breathable, comfortable, and causes less skin irritation than synthetic blends.

432. Shop at the end of the season for your child's wardrobe for next year. You can easily save 75 percent on new clothing. To determine the size to buy, consider what your child's age will be and his growth pattern. Check *75% OFF* with parents who have a child a year older to see what sizes their kids are in.

433. If you decide that you're going to re-sell your baby's clothing when you're finished using it, it is better to stick to name brands. The following brands are top-sellers among online auction shoppers: Gymboree, Gap, Tommy Hilfiger, Ralph Lauren, and Hanna Andersson. However, don't

pay full price for it. Look at discounters like Marshalls, T.J. Maxx, and Ross. Even shop garage sales and secondhand stores.

434. Keep clothing well-organized so you know exactly what you have in each size. That way, you won't forget you have something until baby has outgrown it or needlessly buy a replacement item. Keeping the next size up ready to go in the closet can help.

435. If you get too much infant clothing as gifts, exchange them for bigger sizes right away. If you wait to return them, chances are they'll get marked down or cleared out, which makes an even exchange much more difficult. Sometimes the store will only give you store credit in the amount of the current selling price, which, if you wait, could be just a fraction of the original price.

436. Be sure to wash items before the time comes when you think your child will fit into a certain piece of clothing. Some items will shrink in the wash and be too small for your child to wear.

437. When buying two-piece pajamas, buy more than one of the same style. That way if one piece becomes damaged or stained, you can still wear the remaining piece with the other set.

WORTH IT

438. When shopping for blanket sleepers, buy the ones without the feet. You will find that they fit your child a lot longer.

439. When buying clothing, consider how easy it will be to get it on your baby. Choose zippers over buttons, and avoid anything that

has to be pulled over baby's head. Clothes that are difficult to get on tend to sit in drawers unused.

440. Search eBay for gift cards and merchandise credit slips from your favorite national clothing retailers. Use keywords like "gift card," "credit," "certificate," "voucher," etc.

441. Spring merchandise is least expensive in late June. Look for sales to be the best a week or so before the Fourth of July holiday.

442. Summer clothing hits rock-bottom prices in September, with markdowns starting at 50 percent right after Labor Day. If you wait until the end of September you can find merchandise for 75 percent off or more.

443. Fall and winter clothing is cheapest in January. Stores will typically mark their merchandise down to 50 percent off right after Christmas. It will go down to 75 percent off or more by the end of January. Shoppers who can wait until February may find even better deals, but selection will be very limited.

444. For kids that are especially rough on clothing, consider buying corduroy. Corduroy is more durable than denim and holds up well over time.

445. If sweaters start to show pilling, shave them gently with a disposable razor.

446. If you plan on having more children, try to buy gender-neutral clothing as much as possible. Shop in the boys' section to get

clothing that is more durable, and in some cases less expensive. Plus, it is easier to get away with dressing a little girl in blue than it is to dress a boy in anything feminine.

447. If you know how to sew, consider making some clothes for your baby. There are many patterns available that you can use over again as your baby grows and changes sizes. Look for free patterns online or make your own patterns from existing items in your baby's wardrobe.

448. *Always* save your receipts. If an item falls apart too soon or shrinks too much the first time you wash it, bring it back to the store with receipt in hand. Most retailers will refund your money on defective merchandise. Keep them in an accordion caddy (available at most dollar stores) sorted by store name to make it easier.

socks and shoes

449. Don't spend a dime on baby shoes until your child has learned how to walk. Shoes are unnecessary for a child who hasn't learned to walk yet. If you're concerned with keeping your child's feet warm, invest in an inexpensive pair of slippers or soft-soled leather booties.

450. Bathtub decals placed on the bottom of your baby's slippers will prevent him from slipping on smooth surfaces like hardwood floors.

451. When buying socks for your baby, buy white socks all in the same brand. That way, if you lose one, the remaining sock can be paired with another one. Many moms rave about Old Navy antiskid socks. The sizes are noted right on the bottom, preventing you from matching two odd-sized socks.

452. Instead of buying socks with the anti-skid sole, which can cost double or triple the price of plain socks, make your own with puffy fabric paint. A little bottle of fabric paint costs about $2 (the price of one pair of antiskid socks) and will last several seasons. Be creative—write your child's initials on the bottom, the size of the socks, or just cute little designs!

WORTH IT

453. Don't buy too many dresses for your six- to twelve-month-old daughter. At this age, she will be crawling or rolling around, and dresses just get in the way. Instead, stock up on sturdy leggings.

454. Use socks to cover your newborn's hands to prevent scratches rather than buying baby mitts.

REUSE

455. Stride Rite shoes have long been considered the standard in high-quality baby shoes. However, a new pair can set you back as much as $50. Stride Rite also manufactures shoes for Target and Sears for much less. The Sears brand is called Munchkins, and the Target brands are Kid Smart and Baby Smart.

456. If the soles of baby's shoes are too slippery, use a little bit of sandpaper to scuff up the bottoms.

457. Shoes.com offers an easy-to-use shoe measuring system. Visit their website to print their measuring system (a .pdf file) on any standard printer.

FREE

458. If your child's shoelaces lose the tip, you don't need to replace them just

yet. Try coating the ends with a coat of clear fingernail polish, and you should be able to thread it through the eyelet again.

459. A toothbrush can help clean the threads and lint that get stuck in Velcro shoe closures.

460. The Mr. Clean Magic Eraser takes away scuff marks from baby's white shoes. Baby wipes also work well. Correction fluid can help to cover up a scuff mark if it doesn't come off. For black shoes, use a permanent marker to fill in scuff marks.

winter gear

461. When considering buying a snow-suit or bunting for your baby, make sure it has legs. While the "bag" styles are nice, you

will have a hard time when it comes to getting baby in a car seat.

462. Consider buying an insulated car-seat lining with a zippered cover instead of a heavy winter coat. It eliminates one layer of clothing to have to put on your baby. Dress your baby in layers for added warmth.

463. It is safer to use a car-seat cover than to strap your baby into the car seat with a winter coat on. A bulky coat prevents the seat belt from being tight enough.

getting the most out of baby clothes

464. If you get a stain on a favorite item of clothing, cover it with a cute sew-on appliqué or iron-on transfer, making sure they are attached securely. If the whole thing has been

stained, tie-dye it! You can even create coordinating sets (from clothing that previously didn't match) with this technique.

465. Cut off the leg holes of a onesie to make a T-shirt that will fit for several more months. If it's cotton it shouldn't even need hemming.

REUSE

466. Make "baby legs" from a pair of knee-high socks by cutting off the foot of the sock. You can leave the edge raw or finish it with a knit band made from the foot of the sock. It's a great way to reuse socks with holes.

REUSE

467. You don't have to spend a lot on a trendy baby boutique onesie for your little one to make a fashion statement. Instead, make your own with iron-on transfer paper that can

be found in big-box office supply stores. Simply find a funny or witty graphic, saying, or logo and print it onto the transfer paper using your computer and printer. Place it face down on the onesie or T-shirt and apply heat and pressure with your iron according to the directions.

468. Cut the feet off tights that your baby girl has outgrown and turn them into leggings. If you know how to sew, you can add lace or ribbon at the bottom.

469. Make hair accessories for your baby girl by hot-gluing your own embellishments onto a plain clip or headband. Ideas include ribbons, ricrac, beads, buttons, pom-poms, silk flowers, or fabric.

470. Prolong the life of your child's snap-crotch garments by using clothing extenders. Extenders have snaps on both ends that fit most bodysuit brands and add about four inches of length to onesies and rompers for longer wear. They can be ordered from One Step Ahead by visiting their website and searching for "Garment Extenders": www.onestepahead.com.

471. When your little girl outgrows one of her favorite dresses in length but it still fits on top, pair it with leggings and wear it as a top.

472. If your baby son outgrows the length of his pants before the waist, you can cut them off to make shorts.

473. Preemie and newborn clothing can be saved and used as doll clothes. (REUSE)

474. Add a layer of lace to dresses and pants that become too short for your little girl. Make sure you prewash the lace or ribbon before sewing.

475. When your baby is learning to crawl, avoid worn-out knees by making knee pads. You can make them by cutting a few inches off a tube sock. Not only do they save your child's clothing from wear and stains, they help protect little knees, too!

476. If your baby girl outgrows the length of her pants before the waist, you can cut them off and make them into capris. This works especially well with jeans. Just cut off the pants at the

appropriate length, wash to create a fringe, then sew a cute decorative ribbon around the bottom. You can even embellish stains or spots with matching appliqués or bows.

477. When your baby outgrows her blanket sleepers, cut the feet off.

478. Don't put those cute tees and short-sleeve shirts away when the weather gets cold. Instead, invest in a couple basic long-sleeve tees to wear underneath them ($3 to $4 at Wal-Mart).

WORTH IT

479. The sleeves of an old adult sweatshirt can be cut off and turned into pants for your baby or toddler. Sew the sleeves together and add elastic to form a waistband.

REUSE

where to shop and when

the children's place

480. The Children's Place does deep markdowns. Separates like tees, pants, shorts, and shirts can often be found at the end of the season for $2.99 or less.

50-75% OFF

481. The Children's Place has a credit card. Cardholders get 10 percent off purchases for the first twelve months as well as earn points. They also have a birthday club, where members can sign up to get a gift coupon on their child's birthday.

the gap

482. Wednesdays are a great day to shop The Gap since they typically do markdowns midweek. Ask your local store when they do theirs. The Gap's final markdowns always end in the number 7. So if an item is marked $4.99, you know it will go down at least one more time. If it is $3.97, you know that is rock-bottom and you better grab it!

483. If you are a regular Gap shopper, save your receipts. If you stop by their store within two weeks of making a purchase, they will give a price adjustment for clothing that has

been marked down within that time. It isn't necessary to bring the clothes, just the receipt.

484. Gap Credit Card holders receive an additional 10 percent off their purchases the first Tuesday of each month. For every $200 purchased with the Gap card, you get *10% OFF* $10 in merchandise vouchers.

485. If you see something on sale at baby-Gap but not in the right size, have the manager check other stores in your area or on the Web. To avoid the shipping charge, you merely need to order one item at regular price (a pair of socks, for example). Your merchandise is mailed right to your door within a few days.

old navy

486. It is hard to beat Old Navy's clearance racks for cute kids' clothes at reasonable prices. Because they like to turn over their inventory every six weeks, their clearance racks are often stocked with items for $4.99 and under. They occasionally will have items for $0.97 and $1.97. Like The Gap, they typically do their markdowns midweek.

487. Sign up for the Old Navy credit card and get a $10 merchandise voucher for every $200 you spend in their family of stores (The Gap, Banana Republic, and Old Navy), plus other coupons and discounts.

488. Old Navy's price adjustment policy is fourteen days. Bring your receipt back to the store within that period of time to receive a credit for the difference in price.

gymboree

489. Gymboree's clothing lines are coordinating and buyers collect pieces to mix and match. For that reason, their clothing is one of the best out there for resale. In-demand items that have been very gently worn occasionally sell on eBay for more than the original retail price!

490. Wait for Gymboree's Circle of Friends Sales (30 percent off) and Gymbucks periods (buy $50, get $25 to spend later) to shop. Combine these sales with clearance merchandise, and you can save quite a bit.

$25

491. If you don't see what you like in the front of the store, ask an associate if they have any merchandise in the back (this is typically the merchandise that's been discounted the most).

Sometimes they'll move past lines off the sales floor to make room for newer, full-price lines.

492. Sign up for the Gymboree Visa card and get an additional 5 percent off your purchases there. Gymboree Visa holders also receive added benefits such as additional discount days, advance notice of sales, and a merchandise voucher when they sign up for the card.

5% OFF

493. Gymboree's price adjustment period is fourteen days. If you buy an item of clothing that gets marked down within fourteen days of your purchase, bring in your receipt for a credit of the difference. There's no need to bring in the merchandise itself.

494. When you're at your local Gymboree store, ask the associate if you can sign

up for their mailing list. You will get advance notice of special sales and reminders to use your Gymbucks.

495. For serious Gymboree addicts, check out the Gymbohaven website. You'll find information on upcoming sales and outlet openings as well as photographs of past and present Gymboree clothing lines: www.gymbohaven.com.

other baby clothing retailers

496. T.J. Maxx, Marshalls, and Ross are great places to find deals on name-brand children's apparel. They offer the same brands as department stores for 20 percent to 50 percent off.

497. Kohl's is another retailer to check out, but never pay full price there. Shop during sales and when they issue Kohl's Cash

(earn a $10 voucher to spend later for every $50 spent). Kohl's cardholders also earn discounts such as an extra 15 percent to 30 percent on merchandise at certain times during the year.

$10

498. Join the Sears KidVantage program. Sears will replace clothing that has worn out with the exact same size and brand when you are a member as long as you save your receipt. When KidVantage members accumulate $100 or more in sales, they receive a certificate good for 15 percent off regular and sale merchandise. Membership is free.

15% OFF

499. Target typically marks their kids' clothing down on Mondays. They usually start at 30 percent, then go to 50 and 75 percent if items don't sell. If you're lucky enough to hit their store when a bunch has just been marked down to 75 percent off, stock up! At that discount, their clothes are cheaper than garage sale prices.

500. Like Sears, ShopKo stores also have a wear-out guarantee on their clothing. Their Kid-Tough policy states that if your child rips, tears, or ruins a garment before she outgrows it, ShopKo will replace it in the same size for free.

FREE

501. Kmart and Wal-Mart also offer low everyday prices on clothing basics.

outlet shopping

502. Clothing with cut tags or black marker through the label found at outlets are taken from the regular stores' inventory. Other clothing may be specially made for the outlet, or of a slightly lower quality.

503. Carter's, famous for their durable sleepwear, has outlet stores across the country. Shop the racks in the back for sleepwear at $7

and $10 per set. Some merchandise is irregular, but will be noted on the tag. Visit their website to join their celebration club to receive coupons: www.carters.com.

504. Healthtex outlets are found in conjunction with Vanity Fair outlets across the country.

505. Oshkosh outlets are a great source for quality kids clothing at reasonable prices. Wait to shop their clearance sales, which are held at the end of each season. Clothing can be found at prices 50 percent to 75 percent off retail. Give the cashier your address and email information to receive coupons for additional savings.

75% OFF

506. Gap Outlet stores carry merchandise from previous seasons along with

clothing made exclusively for the outlet. Most moms report that finding bargains at the outlet is hit or miss.

507. Old Navy Outlets carry their own "Outlet" line of clothing, which is indicated on their tags. Their prices are less than what you'd find in their regular stores. However, you probably won't be able to do any better than the clearance racks in their regular stores.

508. The Children's Place Outlet stores are definitely worth a visit. For the best deals, search the clearance merchandise at the back of the store. Some moms have been lucky enough to find items under a dollar.

509. Gymboree also has outlet stores all across the country. They carry clothing and accessories made especially for their outlet stores.

Because they are made without many of the intricate details and embellishments as the lines in their typical mall stores, they can sell them at discounted prices. Because the outlets don't participate in the same great sales as regular Gymboree stores (see tips #489–495), bargain hunters are often better off shopping at the mall stores.

510. Visit the Outlet Bound website to search for outlets by store and by location: www.outletbound.com.

buying online

511. Check out Yahoo! Groups and search for discussion loops for infants' and children's resale clothing. By joining a discussion group, you receive messages via email from other members related to buying and selling new or gently used children's clothing. Search keywords such as the

brands of clothing you prefer, "resale," or "clothing": www.yahoogroups.com.

512. Look for online consignment and thrift stores such as www.resale.net and www.handmedowns.com that sell gently used kids' clothing.

513. Subscribe to the online newsletters of the clothing stores you like. They will inform you of their sales and often email coupon codes good for free shipping or other discounts.

514. Always check to see if online coupon codes are available to use on your online order. Visit Mommysavers.com for a complete listing of current codes: www.mommysavers.com.

tips for online auctions

515. Taking advantage of misspellings, typos, and human errors can help you find some great auction deals. Because some auctions include inaccuracies that make them hard to find in searches, very few people actually bid on them. There are even sites strictly devoted to helping you locate these "hidden" deals, like www.hiddenauction.com and www.fatfingers.com.

516. Ask questions. Most items can't be returned, so you'll want to make sure you ask about the condition and size before you place your bid. If anything is vague or omitted, write to the seller and ask before placing your bid.

517. Check the seller's feedback rating. The comments under his or her

feedback profile should be able to tip you off to a disreputable seller.

518. Check shipping costs before placing your bid. Sometimes the high cost of shipping can negate any savings. Be sure to read the seller's return policies as well.

519. Look for clothing in lots, or groups of more than one item, to save money. You can even purchase an entire wardrobe for your child at considerable savings.

520. Be sure to note the condition of the clothing, whether it is used (and how used) or new with tags on (NWT). If the clothing is used, any stains or other problems should be carefully noted.

521. When buying on eBay, check the seller's other auctions. You may be able to take advantage of combined shipping costs to save money on additional items.

522. Wait as long as possible to place your bid. Otherwise, you will drive up your own price. There are even online services that will place your bid for you in the last seconds of the auction for a small fee, such as www.auctionsniper.com and www.powersnipe.com.

resale shopping and garage sales

523. Mondays and Tuesdays are the best days to shop thrift stores. Most stores receive more donations on the weekend, and put out their new merchandise early in the week.

524. Check to see if your neighborhood thrift stores have "bag sales" (where everything you can stuff in a paper bag is just $5) or half-off days.

50% OFF

525. Once Upon a Child is one of the leading children's resale shops in the country. Their stores are independently owned, and are stocked with high-quality used clothing at reasonable prices. To find one near you, visit their website at www.ouac.com. Other resale stores include Kid to Kid (www.kidtokid.com) and Children's Orchard (www.childrensorchard.com).

526. Visit the National Association of Resale & Thrift Shops website to find thrift stores in your area. Click on "shopping guide" and enter your zip code: www.narts.org.

527. Thethriftshopper.com is a national online directory of neighborhood thrift stores. The site allows visitors to rank stores on a scale from one to five on criteria such as price, selection, and cleanliness—meaning savvy shoppers get the inside scoop on the best stores in their area: www.thethriftshopper.com.

528. Garage sales are far and away the most economical way to find kids' clothes at bargain prices. Most kids' clothing is 75 to 90 percent off the original price.

529. Be careful when buying ahead, taking the amount of storage space you have and styles into consideration. Trendy pieces look dated after a couple of years and you'll be using valuable storage space to keep it at home. A good rule of thumb: don't buy anything that won't be worn within a year's time.

530. Location, location, location. Looking for garage sales in wealthier neighborhoods increases your chances of finding high-quality items. On the flip side, don't avoid lower-income neighborhoods if they are advertising items that you need. You may be surprised at the great deals you find.

531. Neighborhood garage sales are great because you can go to many sales without having to drive. Bring a friend when hitting neighborhood garage sales and split up. Give each other a copy of the items on your list and shop for each other. Carry your cell phones so you can communicate if questions arise.

532. When the garage sale ads come out, map out your route according to addresses and starting times. If you're really into garage sales, have your neighborhood/hometown

map laminated. That way you can mark addresses each week and wipe them off when you're finished.

533. Get to the sale when it starts, or even a little bit early. The "good" items are always the first to go, so it pays to be one of the first through the door.

534. Bring a few sets of AA, C, and D batteries and a mini screwdriver along in your purse. That way you can test electronic toys to see if they work.

535. If you are lucky enough to hit a sale that has clothing in the exact sizes you need, is of high quality, and is priced right, ask them to call you before their next sale. They may even let you shop early, allowing you to get the best selection. If you're even luckier, you can negotiate buying

the whole "lot" of clothing at a reduced price. That saves the seller the time of organizing and pricing her items—you both win!

536. If you're at a good garage sale and are looking for a certain item that you don't see, a snowsuit for example, don't be afraid to ask. Sometimes the seller will have what you want, but didn't get around to pulling it out and marking it for the sale.

537. Make sure you check the zippers, buttons, and snaps on clothing you purchase. These items will end up never being worn if they are defective. However, if you don't mind mending, point out the flaw to the seller and ask for a discount.

538. Go a bit later after the big crowds have dissipated. The sellers are usually willing to make a deal on what is left.

539. If you don't like a price, particularly on a big-ticket item, don't be afraid to offer them less than what they're asking. This strategy is much more effective at the end of the sale, when the seller is more willing to make a deal.

540. When you find several items you want to purchase, make a single offer for the entire lot. The seller more often than not agrees to the price you offer.

laundry and cleaning up

caring for baby clothing

541. Use a zippered pillowcase as a laundry bag for your baby. Throw the whole thing in the washer and dryer.

542. Make your own laundry soap at home. Combine half a bar of grated Fels-Naptha soap with two pints water. Heat the mixture on low until it's melted. Stir in half a cup of borax and half a cup of washing soda (found in the laundry

aisle) and remove it from the heat. Pour the mixture into a large bucket and add enough water to make two gallons. Let the mixture stand overnight until it thickens. Use one cup per load.

543. When buying laundry detergent, consider the cost per load. Because the amount of detergent needed for a load can vary by brand, the price per ounce isn't a reliable measure of the true cost.

544. Wash items containing polyester inside out to reduce pilling and fuzzing.

545. Carry a stain-stick in your diaper bag. That way you can pretreat a stain when it occurs, making it easier to get out in the wash once you're home.

546. Laundry detergents formulated just for babies are not necessary. Most babies are not bothered by the detergents used by the rest of the family. If your baby does react to stronger detergent, it may be a sign the clothes weren't rinsed well enough. Try running the rinse cycle twice to remove all traces of detergent, or try regular detergents that are fragrance-free.

547. Use a lingerie bag for baby's dirty socks. It can just be tossed in the washer, then you won't lose any of those little socks and it will be easier to match them up. Keep one in the laundry basket and put the socks in it as they get dirty.

548. Use vinegar instead of fabric softener when washing baby clothes. It is much less expensive than commercial fabric softeners and better for your baby's skin. Make sure you use white vinegar.

549. Proper care of your baby's clothing will extend its life and help it bring a higher price if you plan on selling it when it has been outgrown. Be sure to pretreat stains and wash "special" outfits in cold water to minimize fading.

stain removal

550. Commercial stain removers most recommended by moms include Totally Toddler spray, Oxiclean Baby, and Zout.

551. Make your own stain pretreater by mixing one part laundry detergent, one part hydrogen peroxide, and one part water in a spray bottle. Spray stains and rub the material together or scrub it with a soft brush (such as a nail brush or a toothbrush) if needed.

552. To remove formula or other baby stains from baby's white clothing, try the Clorox Bleach Pen. It allows you to apply bleach on a small area of the garment without getting it on the entire piece of clothing.

553. Soak protein-based stains like milk and feces in cold water. Hot water cooks the protein, causing it to coagulate on the fabric's fibers and making it hard to remove.

554. Never put a stained garment in a dryer. The heat from the dryer can set the stain.

555. Fresh formula stains can be removed by using a little meat tenderizer. Mix the tenderizer with water to create a paste, dab it on the

stain, and leave it on overnight. The meat tenderizer will eat away the formula stain, which is a protein.

556. Hydrogen peroxide can be used to remove formula stains and yellowing of old garments. Mix a solution of one part hydrogen peroxide with one part water. Soak the clothes for about half an hour. If the stain is still there, add a little more peroxide and soak the garment for another half hour. Launder as you normally would.

557. Murphy's Oil Soap can also be used for removing formula stains. Apply a small amount to the stain, and gently rub it with a toothbrush. Wash the garment as you would normally.

558. Baby feces can be removed from clothing by soaking in an enzyme solution such as Biz detergent with a little water. The enzymes eat away the garment stains.

559. For your toughest stains, make a mixture using one cup of laundry detergent, half a cup of bleach, one-quarter cup of dishwasher detergent, and one gallon warm water. Soak heavily soiled items overnight, then machine wash them.

560. Vomit can be removed from clothing by using a mixture of cold water, one quart of ammonia, and a little detergent.

561. Liquid dish soap is an effective stain remover. It breaks down the tough protein-type stains like feces, baby food, and formula.

cleaning other items

562. For items that can't be laundered, clean them with baking soda. Sprinkle baking soda on a damp sponge and use it to clean high chairs, car seats, strollers, and other baby gear.

563. Crayon can be removed from your walls with WD-40. It can also be used to remove crayon stains from clothing. Just spray it on as you would a stain remover, and launder as usual.

564. The powerful hoses they have at car washes are great for cleaning baby items like strollers, exersaucers, outdoor toys, and other baby gear.

565. Clean baby's toys with a mixture of four tablespoons baking soda to one quart warm water. Disinfectant spray works well on toys that have tiny parts and crevices.

* PART FIVE *

the newest
room
in the house

* chapter 13 *
# bedding and furniture bargains

bedding

566. When purchasing bedding for your first child, choose a gender-neutral color or pattern. Subsequent children will be able to use it regardless of their sex. You can always accessorize in pink and blue.

567. Don't buy bedding as a part of a set. You will be paying for items you don't really need: a comforter, a diaper stacker, bed ruffle, etc. It is a better bet to buy what you need separately.

568. Bed, Bath and Beyond is a well-known source for towels and sheets, but many parents don't realize they also carry cribs and baby bedding. First-time newsletter subscribers receive a 20 percent coupon to either use in-store or online, which can add up to big savings on a major purchase like a crib. Visit www.bedbathand-beyond and click "Email Signup."

(20% OFF)

569. Invest in high-quality crib sheets. Look for at least two to three sheets in 100 percent cotton. They will see more wear and tear than your own sheets, and you'll want ones that will withstand the repeated washings.

(WORTH IT)

570. If you want to do the eco-friendly thing, it's especially budget-friendly to remember that less is more. The only bedding you really need to buy specifically for baby is crib sheets. By skipping the other matching pieces you

can afford to spend more for organic sheets that are free from bleaches and dyes. Great places to shop for organic bedding include www.babiesrus.com and www.babyearth.com.

571. When buying baby's layette, skip the comforter. Babies should not be put to sleep with bulky bedding because it can increase the incidence of SIDS. Invest in a nice blanket instead.

572. Pick a pattern with commonly found colors. If you choose bedding in a strange pattern, you'll have trouble finding accessories to match it.

573. If you're handy with a sewing machine you can easily make your own baby accessories. Bed ruffles, diaper holders, and curtains often come in fabric-panel form at the fabric

store, making sewing a breeze. You just have to be able to sew a straight seam.

574. Buy enough fabric to make bedding for a twin-sized bed. That way when your baby graduates to a "big" bed, you won't have to completely redecorate her room.

575. If you fall in love with a certain pattern, search for it by keyword on eBay. You may be able to find the exact same thing at substantial savings. EBay doesn't always mean used, either. Enter keywords such as "NWT" (new with tags) or "NIP" (new in package) if it's new bedding you're looking for.

576. Consignment stores, online classifieds such as Craigslist, thrift stores, and garage sales often have baby bedding for a

fraction of the price of new sets. Look for solid colors that match your room décor.

577. If you know how to sew, you can use your own worn sheets to make baby sheets, using the less-worn part. Or, purchase used sheets at garage sales and thrift stores for this purpose. They will be nice and soft!

REUSE

578. Keep your receipt when buying crib sheets. If they shrink too much to fit properly, return them. Sheets that come loose pose an entanglement risk to your baby.

579. It's not only unnecessary to use a bumper pad for your crib, it can be dangerous. The ties that secure it to crib bars can pose a safety hazard to your baby. If you do use a bumper pad, trim off excess length after tying to prevent your baby from becoming entangled in the ties.

580. Overstock.com has a steady supply of crib bedding at up to 75 percent off the retail price. Check back at frequent intervals until you find a pattern you like. Their shipping is reasonable, too.

75% OFF

581. Off-price retailers like T.J. Maxx, Marshalls, and Ross are another source for baby bedding and accessories. They often carry designer and name-brand labels at up to 60 percent savings.

60% OFF

582. Target also has great baby bedding at reasonable prices. Be sure to check the endcaps in the baby department for clearance merchandise, which can sometimes be found for 75 percent off. If you find only a few pieces of what you want on clearance, ask their customer service department to call other stores in your area to locate the matching ones.

75% OFF

583. Skip the sleep positioner. They are designed to keep babies on their back while asleep, reducing the rate of SIDS. If a baby is able to roll from back to tummy his rate of SIDS is greatly reduced anyway, leaving no reason to make him sleep on his back.

584. Whatever pattern you choose, make sure it doesn't have too much white in it. White gets dirtier faster, and can discolor with a lot of washing.

furniture

585. Choose furniture that will easily make the transition from infancy to childhood. By selecting pieces that are appropriate for any age, you will save time and money by not having to purchase more later.

586. You don't have to stick to baby stores to find furniture for your infant. Most regular furniture stores and outlets carry a selection of nursery furniture.

587. A bookcase is a must-have item for your nursery. Your baby will accumulate lots of books, and you'll want a place to display them. Invest in one that can be used as your child grows older. Be sure to anchor it to the wall to avoid it accidentally tipping over.

WORTH IT

588. Craigslist.org is a good place to find gently used furniture available for local pickup. In some cases, it may even be worth the drive to a neighboring community. Check their site frequently, since good deals get snapped up quickly (sometimes within an hour of when they're posted).

589. Check out IKEA for good prices on quality kids' furniture. This Swedish-based retailer has opened many stores in the United States in recent years, and chances are there's one close to you. Because the furniture requires assembly, they are able to offer great prices.

590. Refinishing or stripping furniture is a great way to extend the life of old pieces—but it should be left up to another family member, not the expectant mom. Most chemicals used in refinishing are highly toxic and could be dangerous to you and your unborn baby.

591. Make sure all used furniture you purchase for your baby is splinter-free. Also steer clear of furniture with sharp edges or corners, or bolts or other protruding hardware.

592. Save up to 50 percent buying unfinished furniture and painting or staining it yourself. Be sure to use a nontoxic finish. Look in your yellow pages or do a search on the Internet for stores in your area.

50% OFF

593. Instead of a toy box, consider buying a large hamper or wicker basket. You can use it for toys now and other kinds of storage later.

REUSE

594. Create an occasional table by taking a large plastic garbage can, cutting a wooden plywood circle for the top, and draping it with a large tablecloth or coordinating fabric. Use the inside of the garbage can to store blankets, linens, or outgrown clothes.

595. Buy used furniture and refinish or paint it so all of the pieces match. Furniture painted with enamel has the added benefit of being easy to clean. Add new knobs or drawer pulls to complete the look.

jazzing up the walls and windows in baby's room

wall decorations

596. Resist the urge to wallpaper your nursery. Paint is one of the least expensive ways to decorate a room, and can be changed easily as your child gets older. If you're set on wallpaper, do a border instead of the entire wall. A border is less expensive and is easier to remove.

597. When painting, use "oops paint"—paint that has been tinted the wrong color. You can usually purchase a can for a few dollars (compared to $15 to $25 a gallon for premium paints) and you can still tint it the color of your choice.

80% OFF

598. Instead of hiring a professional painter/artist to design murals on your nursery walls, try doing it yourself at home. There is an easy way, regardless of whether you possess any artistic talent or not. Find a picture that you want to paint on the wall and take it to your local print shop and have a transparency made. Rent or borrow an overhead projector, and project the image on the wall where you want it placed. Pencil in the design, then paint over it.

599. Consider hiring a college art student to paint a unique design or mural on your nursery walls. They're enthusiastic about sharing their talents and even more excited to earn a buck.

600. If you do decide on a hand-painted mural, opt for a design that isn't too babyish. You will want the option of keeping it intact as your baby grows older.

601. A sky effect is a popular paint treatment for nurseries and can be done either on walls or the ceiling. Apply a coat of flat blue paint as a base. Using a four-inch decorator's brush, apply white brushstrokes at forty-five-degree angles. Go over them again with white paint with a smaller two-inch brush to further define cloud shapes. Cover it with a wash of six parts water to one part white paint to soften the edges and create a translucent finish.

602. While today's latex paints are safer than lead-based paints of a generation ago, you should still steer clear of inhaling noxious paint fumes while pregnant. Enlist the help of your spouse, another family member, or friend when it comes to painting your nursery.

603. Instead of using wallpaper over your entire wall, consider using Wallies cutouts. Their border cutouts can be arranged in a linear way to look like a border or they can be used individually on craft projects and furniture. Larger cutouts can be used as murals. They are less expensive than wallpaper, and are more easily removed.

604. A cute look for your walls can be created using inexpensive fabric and liquid starch. Purchase fabric with the characters or pattern that matches your décor, and cut out the shapes you want to use. Mix two teaspoons of starch

and one cup of water. Soak the fabric in the starch solution, then place it anywhere you want on the walls. When you move or get tired of the characters you simply take them off. No mess or stains!

605. Have vinyl letters in any font made to decorate the nursery. Use baby's name, favorite poems, songs, or quotations. They are easy to apply and can be removed easily without damaging the wall. Consider hosting an e-party to earn them instead of paying full price. Check out these sites: www.quotethewalls.com and www.wallwords.com.

606. If vinyl lettering isn't in your budget, the same overhead projector technique as described in tip #598 can be done with fonts and lettering. Or, use a stencil and acrylic paint.

607. Use bath sponges in baby shapes like ducks or teddy bears to create a border. Dip the sponge in paint, dab off the excess, and apply to your baby's wall.

608. Shop online to find great deals on the wallpaper and borders you see at expensive stores. American Blinds, Wallpaper & More has great prices and makes it easy to find what you're looking for. Search by book name, pattern or item number, or keyword. Save up to 25 to 85 percent off most retail store prices. You can find them at www.americanblinds.com.

85% OFF

609. Get older siblings involved in decorating baby's room by using their handprints as a border. Paint the older child's hand and then strategically place her "prints" around the top or midsection of their room as a border. Or, have

friends and relatives do their handprints and sign their name underneath. Paint a horizontal line under the handprints for a more finished look.

window treatments

610. Buy an extra sheet or dust ruffle in your pattern of choice, and use it to make coordinating curtains.

611. For a no-sew valance, drape a light-weight fabric around a curtain rod. For a feminine edge use a fabric like tulle. A fishing net looks cute for boys. You can even do this without a curtain rod; just secure the fabric above your window using a thumbtack.

612. Stain-resistant carpet or hardwood floors are worth the investment. In the first few years of your child's life, he will be spending countless hours on the floor. Make sure you choose a floor covering that can endure the wear and tear.

WORTH IT

613. An aquarium can double as a nightlight. The bubbling sounds are soothing to baby.

614. Consider installing a dimmer switch in your baby's room. There are certain times when you won't want harsh lighting, including feeding times when you get up with your baby in the middle of the night. Having the ability to adjust the lighting will save money on having to buy additional lamps.

WORTH IT

615. Early in infancy, your baby may have a hard time differentiating between day and night. A room-darkening blind is an inexpensive way to block out sunlight. To finish the look, add a valence that coordinates with baby's room.

616. Consider wall-mounted shelves if you have limited space in your baby's room. This type of shelving is practical not only for babyhood, but for all the things your child will accumulate as she grows older. Ample shelf space leaves enough space on the floor for other items, and play space for your baby.

decorations, accessories, and storage in baby's room

crafty and creative decorations

617. Reuse wrapping paper from your baby shower to make decorative wooden blocks to display in your nursery. Use Mod Podge to adhere paper to wooden blocks found at any craft store. Sand the edges lightly and sponge them with brown paint to give them an antique look. Coat the paper with Mod Podge again to seal it. You can also use leftover wallpaper, scrapbook paper, family photos, or other paper embellishments for this project.

REUSE

618. Don't buy expensive décorating magazines for decorating inspiration. Instead, visit design websites where members post their own photos. Roomzaar.com is one with thousands of them. Search by room, keyword, style, or rating.

619. A decorative ribbon strung across a wall can be used to display cards and photos. Pin them on with clothespins or diaper pins.

620. Outgrown infant clothes can be used as a cute wall decoration using twine and wooden clothespins. Secure both ends of the twine against a wall, in the style of an old-fashioned clothesline. Pin articles of clothing on the twine using the clothespins. You can even paint trees on the wall as a mural on which to hang your "clothesline."

REUSE

621. Use the wrapping paper you received baby gifts in to line your baby's dresser drawers.

(REUSE)

622. A shelf can be made for under $20 using a one-by-six-inch board and wall brackets. Placed a foot or so below the ceiling, it is great for displaying collectibles, stuffed animals, baby blocks, and other small items.

623. Unfinished wooden pieces like shelves, stools, rocking horses, and other accessories can be found at craft stores for great prices. Finishing and staining or painting them yourself can save a lot of money.

624. Antique or heirloom hats, dresses, baptismal gowns, and other outfits are an elegant way to dress up a wall. Hang them from little pegs or hooks.

625. Avoid using only paint swatches in choosing your paint color. Swatches are often too small to get an accurate feel for what the color will look like in your baby's room. Instead, use larger items like articles of clothing, baby bedding, or other accessories. Bring the actual item to the paint store, and they should be able to match it perfectly.

626. Create a display board using a one-by-six- or one-by-four-inch board and clothespins or metal jaw clips. Paint the board to match your décor, and let it dry. Attach the clothespins or jaw clips with nails or a hot glue gun. It's an easy and inexpensive way to create a display of cards, photos, hats, etc. When your child is older, use it to display his artwork.

627. When buying lamps, shelving, and other accessories, purchase items that your child can use as he or she gets older.

628. Making your own mobile not only saves money, it allows you to customize it for your baby or to match your décor. Take a set of wooden cross bars or a metal craft hoop, and hang items from it using fishing line. Use items like laminated photos, small lightweight stuffed animals, silk flowers, etc. Hang the mobile from a hook on your ceiling using decorative ribbon. Make sure that it is out of your baby's reach, and that you remove it once your baby is able to sit up.

629. Use leftover fabric to create a French memo board. Buy a piece of corkboard or foam board and secure the fabric over a piece of batting with a staple gun. Run coordinating ribbons in a diamond pattern over the board.

630. If you have leftover wallpaper, create coordinating accessories using a decoupage medium like Mod Podge. Cut out characters or pictures from the wallpaper and adhere them to lampshades, furniture, stools, or even decorative plates to hang on the wall. *REUSE*

631. Adhere leftover wallpaper to the inside back of a bookcase, or paint it the same color as your wall. It creates visual appeal and helps pull together your theme. *REUSE*

632. Create a custom rug out of carpet remnants. Choose colors that match baby's room and cut the pieces into various shapes patchwork-style and attach them with carpet tape. Attach the entire piece to a rubber rug grip with silicone glue and more carpet tape. *REUSE*

633. Don't forget the ceiling. In the first few months of life, your baby will be spending a lot of time lying on her back. Purchase glow-in-the-dark stars for the ceiling or suspend other interesting objects for your baby to look at.

634. Mosquito netting or tulle draped around the head of baby's crib adds an elegant touch. Since you can often find tulle for just $1 per yard, the entire project costs just a few dollars. Just make sure you remove it by the time the baby is able to pull himself up and grab it.

635. An inexpensive kite can add a lot of color to a child's room. Just hang it on the wall or from the ceiling. Add ribbons in coordinating colors on the tail to enhance the look.

636. Frame one of your favorite baby cards to make a cute picture. Paint the frame to coordinate with the card and your baby's décor.

REUSE

637. Make your own bookends using a couple of stuffed animals. Open the seam in the back, remove a little stuffing, and add pebbles or marbles for extra weight. Reclose the seams.

REUSE

638. Use a favorite baby blanket as an organizational accessory in your nursery. Stitch pockets on the front using coordinating fabric. Attach rings to the back and hang it from the wall. The pockets can be used to hold socks, hats, brushes, or other small items.

REUSE

639. While an infant hamper may be cute, it soon is too small to be practical. All those cute outfits fill it up quickly, leaving you wishing you had invested in a larger hamper. Better yet, keep a laundry basket under the crib for this purpose.

storage and organization

640. If you don't have a separate room for a nursery, resist the temptation to upgrade to a bigger home. Bigger homes don't just mean a bigger mortgage: your expenses will be higher across the board for electricity, maintenance, insurance, and so on.

641. If you can't devote an entire room to a nursery, think outside the box and repurpose an existing space like a dining room, office, or guest room for your little one. Creative uses of screens, draperies, shelves, and room dividers can separate the space.

642. If you have a small room, make use of space under the crib for storage. Make use of vertical space by installing shelves on the wall for books, toys, and other small items.

643. Use baskets for storing toys and toiletries, or use one as a laundry hamper. Purchase wicker baskets secondhand and spray paint them white for a clean new look.

644. To free up extra space, move baby's dresser inside the closet. Because her clothes are so small, there's still space for them to hang above it.

645. To organize baby's closet, consider hanging sweater shelves or shoe organizers for storing baby's outfits. This makes great use of vertical space that would otherwise be wasted when hanging tiny clothes. Plus, you can sort outfits together to make matching them quick and easy.

646. Hang a three-tiered mesh basket from a hook on the ceiling to create more space on dresser tops and changing stations. Use it to store baby wipes or other supplies.

647. A washable area rug is a good investment for baby's room if he's going to use it as a play area. He will be drooling, spitting up, and creating other messes on it.

WORTH IT

648. To organize infant items, hang a clear shoe organizer on the inside door of your baby's closet. It is great for small items like socks, hats, shoes, booties, etc., and you can see them all at a glance. Store little toys and other small items that would otherwise get lost in the closet in the remaining pockets.

649. A net hung in the corner near the ceiling can be a great place to store stuffed animals.

650. Instead of a mobile, hang soft stuffed toys overhead with fishing line from a hook in the ceiling.

* PART SIX *

the wide world of

baby

gear

* chapter 16 *

buying baby gear

gear up or gear down?

651.

Don't be afraid to negotiate with salespeople on high-ticket items. You increase your bargaining power if you are able to buy multiple items from the same store. You may even be able to get a group of parents together (from a childbirth class, for example) to buy together and get a bulk-rate discount.

652. Avoid licensed products. Car seats, strollers, and other baby gear with designer names and characters cost up to 30 percent more than the same thing without them.

653. Consider buying items like exersaucers, bouncy seats, or activity gyms at garage sales, thrift stores, or through online classifieds. These items will be used for a short period of time before they're outgrown, so you won't want to invest too much money.

654. Borrow baby gear from a friend or family member if they are done using it for one child but don't have another child to use it yet. They will most likely be thankful to free up the space for additional storage, and be glad to have someone else put it to good use.

FREE

655. Don't get too emotional when shopping. It is easy to fall in love with all the cute baby things you see at the store. Go with a clear plan and shopping list, and try not to stray from it.

656. Don't trust salespeople to steer you in the right direction. While most salespeople are fairly honest, they are trained to sell you as much as they can.

657. Take the advice of other parents that have "been there, done that." Ask your friends what they liked and didn't like about their stroller, high chair, and other pieces of baby gear. Make use of discussion forums like the ones on Mommysavers.com to get the inside scoop on what to buy and what to avoid.

658. Pay for major purchases with a credit card. Most major retailers can now look up your transaction without a receipt by scanning the item and your credit card.

659. Read product reviews on Epinions .com and on shopping sites like Amazon.com. Don't forget that certain items like strollers and car seats are carried in different fabric patterns, so the reviews pertain to that style only. For more reviews, look at the same item in a different color or pattern.

660. Check out buying guides from the library. *Consumer Reports* publishes a buying guide to baby gear and also publishes new reports on diapers, strollers, and other baby items in their magazine. Be wary of buying guides published in magazines and other places that may be supported

by paid advertising. Because their reviews may not be impartial, you'll need to take them with a grain of salt.

FREE

661. Don't invest in any big-ticket item until you've done a fair share of comparison shopping. Be sure to try out the product and its features as thoroughly as you can. If it folds up, try folding it. Try all the latches, buckles, and other features. As you try them out, you'll begin to develop your own opinions about what is important to you as the end-user. Bring along a notebook to take notes on prices and other features you find important.

662. If you know you are going to use something a great deal, such as a stroller, backpack, etc., do some research and get the best you can find. Yard sale or consignment shop finds are great, but don't skimp or you will end up wasting your money on two or three of them!

663. Check to see how easily you can repair or obtain replacement parts for big-ticket items before making your purchase. Certain brands that are well built may cost more initially, but if they are easily serviced can end up costing you less than cheaper brands. Parts and repairs cost only a fraction of the cost of replacement.

664. Save your receipts and packaging. If anything goes wrong with a major purchase, don't hesitate in taking it back to the store. Without a receipt you don't have much recourse. Additionally, when it comes time for resale your item becomes much more marketable.

665. Keep a file folder with all the baby product/gear manuals, instruction booklets, and warranties. If you ever need to remember how something works, call the manufacturer, or

order spare parts, you'll have everything you need in one handy location.

666. Send in the product registration card. If your purchase is recalled, you'll be contacted by the manufacturer for a replacement or repair kit.

667. Look for items that will serve your baby into childhood. High chairs that convert to boosters, baby furniture that can be used into childhood, and other transitional pieces are all wise investments. The longer your child is able to use a particular item, the bigger bang you'll get for your buck.

WORTH
IT

668. Avoid using layaway if at all possible. While it may seem like a good idea to pay for big purchases on an installment plan, you run

the risk of having the item sell out before you pick it up. When that happens, you may be forced to accept a floor model or forfeit your down payment.

669. If you have an item that has been recalled, you may still have some recourse. The manufacturer can send you a repair kit or even a coupon/voucher to put towards a replacement. For a list of recent recalls, visit this site: http://www.recalls.gov/recent.html.

shopping online

670. Facebook has a marketplace that allows members to buy, sell, give things away, or ask for things they want. If you're a member, use it to search for deals on used baby gear, furniture, or clothing. Enter "Marketplace" in the search box on the main page to find listings near you: http://apps.facebook.com/marketplace/.

671. Check several websites to compare costs. You can use online sites such as BizRate, MySimon, Shopping.com, and Froogle to compare prices of just about anything you can buy online. Shopping-bots search different sites for prices and the site displays the prices together on one page for quick comparison.

672. Many websites don't charge you for sales tax. On a big-ticket purchase this can be a huge savings, even negating big shipping charges. Make sure you find out before making your purchase.

673. EBay has every type of baby gear imaginable. There are some great deals to be found on both new and used items. However, make sure you figure in shipping costs before placing your bid. The size and weight of certain items make shipping costs more expensive.

674. Overstock.com has baby bedding, furniture, strollers, and other baby items in stock on a regular basis. They offer low shipping prices as well, making some of the deals you find on their site especially good finds.

675. Check out Craigslist.org's "baby + kids" section for gently used baby gear, or see what your local online newspaper classifieds have available. If you don't see what you want, post a want ad of your own.

676. Freecycle.org is another great site to check out for used baby gear. Each Freecycle group is headed by a local volunteer, and is designed to keep usable products out of landfills. You may be able to snag something for free, then pay it forward: www.freecycle.org.

677. Look for online codes to use with your purchase. For a listing of online coupon codes, visit Mommysavers.com.

678. Craigslist isn't the only site for online classifieds. Kijiji is another noteworthy site to post want ads and search for gently used furniture, baby gear, clothing, and other things your family may need. Listings are separated by city and state and are completely free: www.kijiji.com.

679. Don't forget to figure in shipping costs when making your purchase. What may seem like a bargain online may not be one at all after costly shipping charges are factored in. If you see an item that doesn't vary by more than a dollar or two either way, consider buying it in the store. The manufacturer most likely has listed a preset cost, and by buying it in the store you'll save shipping costs. Plus, it will make any necessary returns much easier.

safety gear and accessories

680. A yardstick or dowel slid through drawer handles can help prevent your baby from opening them.

681. Pad table corners with foam pipe insulation tubes you can get at any home improvement store. Just slit the tube lengthwise, and you have an inexpensive yet effective way to protect baby from sharp edges. Better yet, remove the table completely until baby is steadier on his feet.

682. Baby-proof your house before you think you'll need to do it. Your child will often surprise you with the things she knows how to get into. Get down on all fours and see things the way your baby would.

683. Keep emergency numbers handy and plainly visible. Make sure anyone who comes into your home to take care of your child knows where important phone numbers are.

684. Ask your friends with older children for any baby-proofing items they may have around which they no longer need, such *FREE* as outlet and doorknob covers, toilet locks, and latches.

685. For a baby learning to crawl, there are so many little things on the floor that are tempting to pick up and put in her mouth. Cover your baby's hands with socks so that she can't pick anything up while crawling around.

686. Drape a towel or blanket over the top of a door so that baby won't be able

to slam his fingers in it. A sock on a doorknob can prevent a child from opening it.

687. Shop for safety latches, outlet covers, and other safety devices at home improvement stores or dollar stores. You can find the same thing for much less.

688. Buy a safety gate from a home improvement or pet store. Chances are you'll spend less at one of these stores than at a baby superstore.

689. Don't use the older baby gates with the accordion-style bars with V-shaped openings. They pose an entrapment and strangulation hazard.

690. If you have cabinets that standard safety latches won't fit, or you just don't want to drill holes in your cabinetry, try self-adhesive industrial-strength Velcro.

691. Instead of purchasing a "choke tube" (a device that tests toys to see if they pose a choking hazard), use an empty roll of toilet paper. It is about the same size as a choke tube, and completely free.

FREE

692. Use hook and eye screws at the top of a door you don't want your child to open. Or attach a bell so that you can hear when it has been opened.

693. If your child loves playing with the buttons on your television or DVD player, use an acrylic panoramic frame as a shield. Frames can

often be found at your dollar store as compared to more expensive shields which can run up to $20.

694. When you're done using your baby gate, lay it flat and use it as a drying rack for sweaters and other clothing.

REUSE

play yards

695. If you don't travel often, you may not need a play yard. They are more often used as portable cribs than they are playpens. Cribs can often be borrowed in hotels free of charge.

696. Don't splurge for the bassinet option on a play yard unless you'll be using it as your primary bassinet or as a changing table (see tip #751). These inserts make it easy on your back when your baby is small. However, you may find it's

not worth spending the extra $30 for the few times you may use it.

697. If the mesh in your play yard becomes torn, use dental floss to mend it. Dental floss is strong, durable, and will often match the mesh of your play yard.

698. Never use an adult bed, water bed, or bunk bed as a temporary bed. Infants can suffocate when their bodies or faces become wedged between the mattress and the wall.

699. A hard plastic swimming pool (that's empty, of course) works great as an outdoor playpen for crawlers.

baby monitors

700. Skip the baby monitor with all the bells and whistles such as video capabilities and movement sensors. They're not necessary, and cost a lot more.

701. Consider whether or not a baby monitor is really necessary for your home at all. Most parents sleeping even several rooms away from their baby are awakened easily when baby cries. If your baby will be sleeping on another level or you will be spending time outside while baby naps, then a monitor will be worth the investment.

702. If you buy a new baby monitor, be sure to save the packaging and the receipt. Some monitors pick up cell and cordless phone signals from neighbors nearby, making it hard

to hear your baby's cries. Have the necessary items for a return in case you need to exchange it.

baby blankets

703. A baby blanket is an item that parents rarely have to spend money on, due to its popularity as a baby gift. Don't spend a dime on one until *after* your baby has arrived and you've received the majority of the gifts you expect you'll receive.

704. Make your own no-sew baby blanket with polar fleece. Since fleece won't fray or ravel, you can simply cut the ends without finishing any seams. Or, create a decorative finish with a blanket stitch or fringe edge. For the blanket stitch, use a coordinating yarn color and loop from one side to the other about a half inch from the edge, hooking the last stitch as you go so there is a line that runs along the top. A fringe edge can be made by cutting lines three inches long about one-quarter of an inch

apart. You can even do a two-tone blanket by layering two different fleeces together and tying fringe from each side together.

rockers and gliders

705. Many people would have you believe a glider rocker is an indispensable item. While they are nice for feedings, a traditional rocking chair, recliner, or a comfortable couch will do just as well.

FREE

706. If you buy a glider, make sure it is one you can incorporate into your décor after you've moved on from nursing or bottle-feeding. A lot of people don't think the traditional models are aesthetically pleasing and shop around for "hipper" or more sophisticated looks. Buy a neutral upholstery pattern, skipping the one that only matches your nursery.

707. Skip the expensive coordinating ottoman if you do buy a glider. A sturdy stool will work just as well, and costs a fraction of the price.

708. If you purchase a rocker, make sure it has arms. It is easy for inexperienced parents to overlook this feature, but you will need something to rest your own arm on when nursing or bottle-feeding your baby.

diaper bags

709. Don't buy a diaper bag before your hospital stay. Formula manufacturers usually give them to hospitals and stock them with samples to give to new parents. If yours doesn't, be sure to ask.

FREE

710. The free diaper bags that hospitals give away are the smaller models, and you may find yourself needing a bigger bag for overnights or longer trips. You may be able to make do with a backpack, duffle bag, or small suitcase you already have for such occasions. Don't buy a bigger bag unless you're sure you're going to use it.

711. Buy a pattern dad will feel comfortable carrying, too. If the diaper bag you select is too feminine, he may be reluctant to tote it around. Lands' End and Eddie Bauer both make masculine-looking bags that can be used later as luggage.

712. Patterns for homemade diaper bags are available for free online. Making your own may not be as difficult as you may think, and allows you to customize the fabric pattern: http://www.make-baby-stuff.com/diaper-bag-pattern.html.

713. Consider buying a soft insulated cooler to use as a diaper bag. Choose a large-sized bag or backpack style with ample room for diapers, wipes, and feeding gear. It will keep your bottles the right temperature, and can be used long after your baby is out of diapers.

WORTH IT

* chapter 17 *

getting around

strollers

714. When you're shopping for a stroller, consider how much you'll be using it. If you're an urban dweller who will be using it on a daily basis, opt for the highest quality stroller your budget allows. If you're only going to be using it for occasional trips for the mall, a nice lightweight or umbrella stroller may be all you need.

715. Search for last year's stroller model. Stores will often offer last year's models at greatly reduced rates to make room for new models. The best time to look for deals is November through January. Often times, the only difference is the fabric pattern. If you can't find one in a store, do a search on the Internet using last year's model year.

50% OFF

716. Consider a carrier instead of a stroller. A front or backpack carrier works well and leaves your arms free to do other things than push a stroller.

717. When shopping for an umbrella stroller, make sure it has a basket underneath and a sun shade. These features only cost a little bit more, but are worth the price.

WORTH IT

718. Don't invest your money in frames that are designed to carry a car seat. Travel systems cost just a bit more, and you have a complete stroller to use when your baby is too big to fit in her infant seat.

719. Before buying a travel system or other large stroller, be sure you test it in the trunk of your car. Too many parents have purchased and assembled them only to find out they don't fit.

720. Only buy a double stroller if you are having twins or will have kids within two years of each other. Not only is it a big expense, it can be hard to maneuver and heavy to take in and out of your car.

721. Instead of buying an expensive double stroller which can run over $100, buy two umbrella strollers and use stroller connections. The umbrella strollers are usually under $20 each and connections can be purchased for about $12. When not in use, the connectors can be easily removed so that the strollers can be used separately.

60% OFF

722. If you have older kids, rethink your decision to buy a double stroller. Instead, purchase a model that allows an older child to stand instead of being strapped into another seat. They're smaller than traditional double strollers and easier for parents to push. Notable models include the Sit-N-Stand by Baby Trend or Caboose by Joovy.

723. Instead of buying a stroller bar with toys attached, attach some of baby's own toys using rings. You can even use shower curtain rings you may already have at home, or look for them at any dollar store or discount store.

REUSE

724. If mosquitoes are a problem in your area, you will probably consider buying an insect net for your stroller. However, a little bug repellent on your baby's clothing will accomplish the same thing without requiring an additional purchase. Be sure to use one that is Deet-free.

car seats

725. Check to see if your county has a program for buying car seats at a reduced rate. Your hospital should be able to provide you with information on whether or not such a program exists in your area.

726. When shopping for a car seat, ask the salesperson if you can test it in your car before buying. Some fit better than others. If this isn't possible, be sure to save your receipt to make a possible return easier.

727. Experts recommend not buying a used car seat unless you know its exact history. Car seats that have been in accidents may have damage to the frame that you can't see or check for. Such damage could compromise your own baby's safety if you were to have an accident.

728. Make sure the upholstery on your car seat can be removed and washed.

729. Your insurance company may offer a program to buy car seats at a reduced rate. It is worth investigating.

730. You can save a little money if you buy one convertible seat to accommodate your baby from birth to forty pounds. However, you'll soon find that an infant-only seat may be easier for you to use and may fit your newborn baby better. An infant-only seat can be carried with you wherever you go without waking a sleeping baby.

WORTH IT

731. Skip the head positioner for car seats if yours doesn't come with one. This stage doesn't last long, a month or two at the most. Instead, roll up a hand towel and place it around baby's head to keep it steady.

732. Don't buy a seat protector or mat to go under your baby's car seat. While they are designed to save the upholstery of your vehicle from any damage, they can compromise the fit of the car seat itself.

733. Visit www.carseatdata.org before shopping for a car seat. This organization has an online database allowing you to see which car seats are most compatible with your make and model of vehicle.

734. Search the Consumer Product Safety Commission (CPSC) database at www.cpsc.gov for recent recalls and news releases regarding baby items. Search by category, brand, or date of recall.

735. The National Safe Kids Campaign is a nonprofit organization dedicated to the prevention of unintentional childhood injury. Their website includes links to child seat inspection stations, product recommendations, and current information on policies and recalls. Visit them online at www.safekids.org.

736. Carseat.org is another good online resource for parents to investigate before purchasing a car seat. Their website includes information on recalls, laws, and regulations regarding car seats.

737. Skip the mirrors that allow you to look at your baby in a rear-facing car seat. They can be dangerously distracting for drivers.

738. If you do invest in a sunshade for baby, look for a big one. Too often standard sizes don't provide enough shade for baby, making them completely useless.

739. Sometimes salespeople will try and sell you an extra base to put in your second vehicle. It isn't always necessary. Most infant car seats can be used without the base, by threading

the vehicle's safety belt through slots in the infant seat itself (check your own seat for instructions). Safety experts have found that the base provides no added protection, and the seat is just as safe to use without it.

carriers and slings

740. A front-pack carrier or sling is great to have. Unlike strollers, they free up your hands to get household chores done and are extremely portable. Look for a model with sturdy construction and enough support for baby's head and body. Be sure to try it on before purchasing. There are big differences in fit between brands. Look for a gently used carrier at consignment stores, garage sales, online classifieds, and on eBay.

741. If you love the outdoors, you may want to consider a baby backpack. These are great from about age six to eighteen months. If you can't find a used one at a thrift store, garage

sale, or resale shop, check a used sporting goods store such as Play It Again Sports. The same goes for a baby bike trailer.

742. Even if you're just a beginning seamstress, consider making your own baby sling. Most only involve sewing just a few straight lines. Patterns and instructions can be found online at http://www.mayawrap.com/n_sewsling.php or at http://crafts.sleepingbaby.net/.

bouncers, swings, jumpers, and walkers

743. A stationary exerciser is a great item to have. However, you can save a lot by buying one secondhand. Used models are frequently seen at resale stores and garage sales. Because of their size they are cumbersome to store, and parents typically want to unload theirs as soon as their baby no longer uses it. If you do purchase a new one, look for one that will grow with your baby. New models

include features for babies learning to walk, extending the time it's useful to you.

744. Most parents will tell you a bouncer or a swing is a must-have. Swings and bouncers pretty much do the same thing: soothe a fussy baby with a swinging or vibrating motion. Buy one or another, but not both.

745. If your baby uses a swing or a vibrating bouncer on a frequent basis, invest in rechargeable batteries. You will use them later for toys or other electronic gadgets.

WORTH IT

746. If you do buy a swing, consider an open-top model that allows you to put baby in and take him out easily without bumping his head. Also, consider whether or not you'll want to transport your swing. If you do, purchase one of the

new compact, portable designs that allow you to fold the swing and take it with you. These features are often worth the additional expense.

747. Don't buy a walker. There have been more accidents with this particular piece of baby gear than any other, most of which occur when baby is sent tumbling down a flight of stairs. They can also be dangerous because they put baby at a higher level to reach things or pull things down on himself. Accidents aside, walkers easily scratch hardwood flooring, scrape walls, and don't always work well on carpeting. You're better off keeping your baby in a stationary exerciser.

748. A jumper is another item to steer clear of. They have been associated with a lot of accidents when their springs have broken or come undone. Not all jumper models will fit your particular door or molding. Instead, buy a stationary exerciser that allows your baby to simulate a jumping motion.

749. A "tummy time" mat isn't necessary either. Instead, use your own  blanket and toys.

baby furniture

bassinets and cribs

750. Don't spend your money on a cradle. They cost more than bassinets, and are harder to move around. Either purchase a bassinet if you're looking for a newborn bed, or go right to a crib.

751. If you're going to be using a bassinet, consider buying a play yard with a built-in bassinet feature. It is less costly than a new

bassinet, and you'll be able to use the play yard for other purposes.

752. Bassinets are handy to keep in your room because you don't have to walk a long way to get baby for nighttime feedings. Since they are typically only used a few months, look for a secondhand model. Again, make sure it meets current safety standards and has never been recalled.

753. Bypass a crib altogether and bring your baby into bed with you, a practice known as co-sleeping. While it does save money, it's not without controversy. The American Academy of Pediatrics doesn't recommend co-sleeping due to concerns about the risk of suffocation. On the other hand, psychologists believe that sleeping in a family bed strengthens a baby's sense of security. Check with your pediatrician before trying this method.

FREE

754. Arm's Reach Products makes a co-sleeping bed the same height as an adult bed that securely links with yours. It costs less than a traditional crib and also converts to a play yard.

755. If you're using a bassinet, there's no need to purchase special sheets or bedding. A standard size pillowcase should fit right over the little mattress. Plus, you'll get to use it long after your baby has outgrown the bassinet.

REUSE

756. An inexpensive crib is just as safe as an expensive model. Because of strict government guidelines, all cribs made in North America must adhere to the same safety regulations. This means that the crib bought at the discount store is just as safe as one purchased in an upscale baby boutique.

757. When shopping for cribs, be aware that some floor models may have screws loose. A rickety crib may simply be an indication that the screws need to be tightened, not that the crib is poorly made.

758. Discounters like Target and Wal-Mart offer cribs at a substantial savings. And since all cribs manufactured in the United States and Canada must meet current safety standards, you're not compromising safety by purchasing an inexpensive model.

759. JCPenney is a source for quality cribs that run a little bit less than furniture stores. You may be able to order it on sale, and have it shipped directly to your home. However, be wary of shipping costs. Most of the time you can save quite a bit by having it shipped to the store and picking it up there.

760. Baby superstores such as Babies "R" Us sometimes offer sales on certain crib models as loss leaders to bring parents into their store. Start watching their sale flyers until you find a model you like that has been significantly reduced. Sign up for their mailing list to receive coupons good for 15 percent off your purchase.

15% OFF

761. Experts advise against purchasing a secondhand crib because a used model may not meet current safety standards. Important pieces of hardware may get lost or get bent, and screw holes can wear out. The glue that holds cribs together deteriorates when they've been stored in super-hot attics or damp basements.

762. When selecting a crib, be sure that you test the crib rail release. Some are easier to manage than others. If you find yourself

stuck with one that is sticky, you're in for a long period of frustration!

763. Look online. Overstock.com occasionally stocks name-brand cribs for up to 50 percent off their retail price. Best of all, their shipping prices are incredibly reasonable. Selection is limited, so start shopping early.

50% OFF

764. Don't buy an odd-shaped or non-standard-sized crib, such as those manufactured overseas. You will find it difficult to find bedding that fits. Even more importantly, it may not conform to the same safety standards.

765. While there are many secondhand baby bargains to be found on eBay, it's likely a crib is not one of them. Because you're unable to inspect the crib yourself before buying, stick to looking for new ones.

WORTH IT

766. You may be able to purchase a new crib on eBay. However, be cautious. Shipping costs may negate any savings you get, and be sure that you are dealing with a reputable seller. Carefully read all feedback comments, and make sure the seller has a long track record of satisfied customers.

767. Let your fingers do the walking. If you find yourself falling in love with a particular crib model, do your homework. Find out the manufacturer and model number. Look up the manufacturer on the Internet, give them a call, and ask if there are other retailers in your area selling the same thing.

768. Cribs with two sliding rails are more expensive than those with one. You really just need one side that slides, since you will likely face one side toward the wall.

769. Your baby doesn't need an expensive mattress. A simple yet firm foam mattress will give baby the support she needs. Because it is lightweight, it will make changing sheets easier.

770. Don't forget to flip baby's crib mattress as you would your own. This will prevent it from getting too much wear in one spot.

771. A mattress pad isn't necessary for your crib. Since crib mattresses are waterproof, there is no need for additional protection from leaky diapers and spit-ups.

772. When your baby is too big for her crib, go right to a regular twin-sized bed and skip the toddler bed altogether. Instead, use safety rails or put the mattress directly on the floor if you're worried she may fall out during the night. In doing so,

you'll save the expense of a toddler bed and have one less transition to go through with your child.

773. When baby outgrows his crib, you can use the mattress as a stow-away bed for children and friends who come to visit. They are easily stored out of sight by sliding under a regular twin-sized bed.

REUSE

774. A crib that converts to a toddler bed may sound like a great idea, but not if you expect to have another baby while your older child is using the converted bed. Also, most convertible cribs require special mattresses, rails, box springs, mattress extenders, and other assembly hardware that cuts into the amount of money you are saving.

high chairs

775. Make sure you buy a high chair that is easy to clean. Avoid cloth upholstery at all costs. Vinyl padding cleans up much more easily.

776. You don't need a high chair with all the bells and whistles. Skip the ones with toys attached, which are harder to clean. Don't buy one with wheels either. Older siblings *love* to push them around, which could cause an accident. Adjustable heights aren't necessary, either. Buy the model with the fewest features that still meets your needs.

777. A reclining high chair isn't a necessary feature, and can even be dangerous. Babies that aren't old enough to be sitting up on their own shouldn't be in a high chair. Feeding a child in a reclined position puts him at a higher risk for choking.

778. Instead of a traditional high chair, consider buying a booster seat that straps onto a dining room chair. It has a removable tray just like a high chair, and can be used without the tray as a regular booster seat when your child is older. It comes apart for easy transport and can even go in the dishwasher. This is a great space-saving solution for apartment dwellers or parents living in tight quarters. Not only that, you can find them for around $25, as compared to $50 to $200 for a high chair.

50% OFF

779. Pay attention to the tray. Make sure it wraps around the baby on the sides; otherwise you'll have extra cleaning up to do. Test it to see how easily it can be removed. Models that can be removed with one hand are particularly nice.

780. Make sure your high chair not only has a safety belt, but that it is one

that has a third strap that goes between baby's legs. Avoid high chairs that have the strap attached to the feeding tray. When the tray is removed, your child isn't protected.

781. Babies tend to slide around in wooden high chair seats, even when they're buckled in properly. Create a nonskid surface for your baby's high chair by cutting rubber shelving paper to fit the seat.

782. A shower curtain liner cut in squares makes a great spill mat to place under your child's high chair. You can also fold up a little piece to keep in your diaper bag to use as a place mat in a restaurant. Look for inexpensive liners at *REUSE* your dollar store.

changing tables

783. It isn't necessary to purchase a changing table. Once your baby is out of diapers, this piece of furniture becomes useless. Most moms will say it is just as easy to change their baby on the floor, on a bed, or in the crib. Or, look for a play yard that comes with a changing table attachment that fits on top with the bassinet. You'll be getting the same thing but spending much less.

784. If you decide you do want a changing table, invest your money in furniture that will stand the transition from baby to childhood. Consider putting your money towards a nice dresser that can accommodate a changing pad on top (to save even more, use a thick folded towel as a changing pad).

785. Be sure that changing tables come complete with safety straps. Even if your baby is strapped onto the changing table, keep one hand on him at all times.

786. Your changing table can be used as a laundry station when you're done with it. Move it to your laundry room and use the compartments to store laundry supplies. The top portion can be used for folding and stacking clothes.

REUSE

787. King-sized pillowcases work well as changing pad covers. When purchased on clearance, they are affordable enough to have plenty on hand.

PART SEVEN

keeping

baby

busy

toys

homemade toys

788. Wrist and ankle rattles are fun for baby and can be easily made at home. First, cut the foot off an old infant sock so that you're left with an elastic cuff. Next, attach some soft, light-weight toys using stick-on Velcro.

789. Socks rolled up can make a great ball for baby to practice throwing. They're soft and easily gripped by little hands.

790. Make your own simple puzzles for baby by gluing snapshots or pictures from magazines onto a piece of sturdy cardboard. When the glue is dry, cut the cardboard into desired shapes. If the cardboard is rough, use an emery board to sand the edges.

791. Plastic measuring cups and spoons are great to use as nesting toys.

792. Use a clear plastic twenty-ounce soda bottle to create an interesting toy for baby. Place objects inside such as aluminum foil balls, pieces of sponge, fabric swatches, glitter, sequins, etc. Fill it with a little water and super-glue the cap on tightly.

793. Make a sock puppet using Dad's worn out gym socks. Make sure you embroider the eyes, nose, and mouth instead of using buttons or other objects that could be choking hazards.

794. Make your own rattle using a clear soda bottle or another small container. Insert objects like beans, unpopped popcorn, pasta, pebbles, or rice. Secure the lid tightly with a little superglue.

795. Make a beanbag with scraps of material and dried beans or unpopped popcorn. Stitch it together securely.

796. Babies love crunching sounds. Take an old tube sock and insert some crinkly cellophane, tin foil, or wrapping paper. Tie off the end and you have a fun toy.

797. Create a "Color Book" for your baby by taking pictures of items around your home in certain colors (for example, red ball, green plant, blue brush, etc.). Better yet, have baby

wear the specific color and pose in the picture as well. Put the photos in a small four-by-six-inch photo album that you can find at a dollar store.

798. Make your own shape sorters. Use cookie cutters to trace two or three different shapes on a coffee can or ice cream bucket lid (cut the holes slightly larger than the trace line). Use the same cookie cutters to cut shapes out of heavy-duty cardboard for baby to insert through the holes.

799. Take several ladies' silk scarves and tie them together end to end, the way a magician would. Insert them into a coffee can and let baby pull them through a hole in the lid.

800. Create an activity board for your infant by attaching simple mechanisms to a sturdy, splinter-free board. Attach things

that snap, roll, click, or make noise. You can find some great things at your local hardware store. Just make sure that they don't contain small parts that could come off and that they're securely attached.

801. Drums can be made from empty formula cans, coffee cans, or ice cream buckets. You can decorate them with contact paper, or leave them as is. Use wooden spoons as drumsticks.

802. Boxes are a great way to keep your baby busy. Cover them with photos and magazine cutouts, and then cover them with clear contact paper. Your baby will enjoy turning the box to different sides and looking at the images.

803. Use large boxes of the same size to make a tunnel for your baby to crawl through. Cut out holes for your baby to peek through and decorate the inside with markers or crayons.

804. Empty lids such as those from shaving cream and hair spray bottles are fun for baby. They enjoy clapping them together, stacking them, and putting things inside them.

805. Plastic cups, bowls, and storage containers are great toys for babies. Put your baby's rattle or another toy in an ice cream or margarine container. She will enjoy shaking it and trying to figure out how to get it out.

806. An old magazine can keep your baby busy for quite some time. Make sure you supervise, as babies like to put things in their mouths.

807. An old set of keys is a great distraction for a fussy baby. Make sure they are clean and sand off any sharp edges.

808. An old computer keyboard can entertain your little one. He will love the clicking noises the keys make. Make sure that you remove any cords and check for loose keys.

809. Make an activity mat for your baby by sewing objects on an old comforter or thick blanket. Sew on some small toys or attach bright pieces of fabric in different textures with Velcro, according to your child's interests and developmental stage.

810. Stuffed animals can be converted to hand puppets by removing the stuffing.

811. An old telephone or remote control is often very entertaining for an infant. They are amused by the buttons and often like to imitate a parent talking on the phone. Be sure to remove all cords and batteries to prevent the baby from injury.

812. Go online. Easy instructions for making homemade infant toys can be found at http://www.make-your-own-baby-stuff.com. Projects include finger puppets, fabric books, blocks, mobiles, and felt toys.

gently used toys

813. For huge savings, buy toys at rummage sales or thrift stores. Your baby won't realize that items aren't brand new. If you're squeamish about germs, disinfect them with a little bleach and water before giving them to your child (expensive nursery sanitizer is unnecessary).

814. Hand-me-down stuffed animals may be infested with mold spores and other allergens. Put them in a tied-off or zippered pillowcase and throw them in the washer on hot to kill any bacteria. If they can't be machine-washed, sprinkle them with a little baking soda or cornstarch

and let them sit for fifteen minutes. Dust or shake off the excess.

815. Buy washable crayons, which wash off walls and clothes with plain water. Also, save broken crayon pieces and make new crayons by heating them in your oven on low in a lined muffin tin just until soft.

(REUSE)

816. When purchasing secondhand toys, make sure you don't have an item that may be dangerous for your child. Visit www .recalls.gov for the complete listing of toys that have been recalled.

817. Make large plastic toys purchased secondhand, such as Little Tikes, look like new with a coat of Krylon Fusion spray paint.

This top-selling paint is the first of its kind that bonds directly to most plastics.

818. Instead of buying new toys, exchange a box of your toys with a box of your friend's or neighbor's toys. If you have a lot of toys, put them into storage and rotate them each week.

FREE

819. Some cities have toy lending libraries available. To search for one in your area, go online and enter the search terms "toy lending library" and your city.

820. The best time of the year to buy toys is January, when retailers are clearing out their unsold Christmas inventory. It isn't

unusual to find popular toys at 50 or even 75 percent off. Try to anticipate which toys you will want your child to have for birthdays and even next Christmas and stock up.

821. Toys "R" Us through Amazon.com runs some great sales throughout the year. January and July seem to be the best months to shop. Look for the "Free Shipping" symbol on certain toys to avoid shipping charges. Parents can read product reviews before purchasing, and avoid paying sales tax.

822. Do not allow babies to play with toys that have missing parts. If you lose a piece to a toy, call the manufacturer. Most will replace the item for free or at cost.

823. An expensive toy box isn't necessary. Wicker baskets, plastic crates, laundry baskets, and Rubbermaid containers all work just as well and can be used for other things after you're done using them to store toys. A plastic garbage can works well to store outdoor playthings and dish tubs work well on bookshelves.

(REUSE)

824. A drawer makes a great toy box, especially in rooms where you need to get work done while baby plays (the kitchen, bathroom, laundry room, etc.).

825. Storage containers that have plastic drawers work well to store toys. Label each drawer by category; for example, rattles, plush toys, etc.

826. Save your ice cream buckets and wipes containers. They work well to store small toys, crayons, and other small playthings.

827. Use plastic shower curtain rings instead of more expensive connecting rings for your baby's toys. You can usually find them at the dollar store. They link together and can be used to hang toys from your stroller or can even be suspended from the ceiling above where you change the baby.

828. Discovery Toys has great toys for babies and young children. Host a party and earn credit towards free products. To find a consultant near you, visit their website at www .discoverytoys.com.

* chapter 20 *
media for your baby—and you!

books, videos, and dvds

829. Borrow movies through an online service like Blockbuster.com or Netflix.com and have them shipped directly to your mailbox (a nice perk for new parents). No late fees apply, plus both services offer a free two-week trial to new members.

830. Rent movies for just $1 through any Redbox kiosk. Redbox features

new DVD releases and typically has a few choices for younger viewers. Search for coupon codes for free rentals on sites like www.redboxcodes.com.

831. Don't buy books with paper pages for your baby. Babies love to rip and chew them, so look for something that will withstand the wear and tear. Board books, fabric books, and vinyl books are better investments.

832. Some board books are really just paper-covered cardboard and the paper will wear off when your baby chews on it. Check the quality of a board book before purchasing by looking at the edges of the pages.

833. Garage sales and thrift stores are great places to pick up books and DVDs for

pennies on the dollar. Consignment and resale shops such as Once Upon a Child also stock books.

834. Your local library can be a great resource for not only books but DVDs, CDs, and even toys. If you don't see what you want on the shelves, request it via your library's system of holds and interlibrary loans.

(FREE)

835. Check to see if your library offers a summer reading program. Many times even infants can participate and earn free prizes.

836. Library book sales are a source for inexpensive used books. Check with your own local public library to see if they have one. Visit the Book Sale Finder website to search for upcoming book sales by state: www.booksalefinder.com.

837. Instead of buying DVDs, record your child's favorite TV programs to watch later. Often the monthly fee for a DVR service is less than a single DVD.

838. Find free sources of entertainment online. Watch full episodes of your kids' favorite shows on the network websites. Or, check out Hulu.com's "Family" Channel and YouTube.com.

FREE

839. Make your own books on tape by recording yourself reading your favorite children's books. Store the tape and book together in a large one-gallon-sized food storage bag.

840. Pick up new or gently used books and DVDs through Amazon.com's Marketplace merchants. Search for books, videos, and

other items through the Amazon website as you usually would. Click on "More Buying Choices" on the product information page for any item you view. When you click the New, Used, Collectible, or Refurbished links, you'll see the selection of products available from Amazon Marketplace sellers.

841. Scholastic Books holds wonderful warehouse sales at special locations throughout the year. Most books are half-price with several bargain areas where paperbacks are as low as $0.50 each. Dates vary by location, and some restrictions apply. Visit their website at http://www.scholastic.com/ bookfairs/events/warehouse/.

842. Visit the Book Closeouts website to find children's fiction and nonfiction books at bargain prices. Check out their scratch and dent section: www.bookcloseouts.com.

843. EBay is a great source for gently used books and videos. If there is a certain theme or character your child enjoys, you can often save by buying them in lots on eBay.

844. Usborne books are educational children's books available through independent sales representatives. You can earn books and other products by hosting a party in your home. To find an Usborne representative in your area, visit their website: www.usbornebooksandmore.com.

free magazines

845. *Baby Talk* magazine, from the same publishers as *Parenting* magazine, offers a complimentary subscription to new parents. To sign up, visit their website at www.babytalk.com.

FREE

846. For a free subscription to *American Baby* magazine, visit their website and fill out a simple form. Your first issue will be on its way within six to eight weeks: www.americanbaby.com.

FREE

847. Bestdealmagazines.com and Magazine values.com are great online sources for inexpensive subscriptions to some of your favorite parenting magazines. Some are as little as $4.69 for a full year's subscription.

entertainment and education

community programs

848. Call your local library to see what programs they offer for children. In addition to story hours, many libraries offer reading programs where kids can earn books and other prizes. Many are available to infants as well as older kids.

(FREE)

849. Check with your community education department to see if they offer

any Early Childhood/Infant classes. Not only are community ed classes a great way to learn about your child's developmental stages, they are a great way to connect with other parents.

850. Check with bookstores in your area to see if they offer programs for children. Many of them offer story hours as well as other activities for children.

(FREE)

851. Gymboree offers a series of parent/child programs devoted to the physical, emotional, and social development of children from infants up to age four. Visit Gymboree's website to print a coupon for a free Play and Music class: www.gymboree.com (click on "Play, Music, and Art Classes").

(FREE)

852. If your child registers for a Gymboree class, be sure to do it during their Gymbuck earning period. In doing so, you'll receive a voucher good for $25 off a $50 purchase at their clothing stores.

$25

playgroups

853. Join a playgroup. A playgroup can provide companionship to both you and your child absolutely free of charge. Several websites can match you with moms in your area:

FREE

* ✳ www.yahoogroups.com

* ✳ www.mommyandme.com

* ✳ www.meetup.com

854. Investigate a membership at your local YMCA. Many offer swimming classes for babies as young as six months of age. They also offer free or discounted babysitting for parents

who use their facilities. You may even be able to get a free membership by volunteering to teach a class or help out at the membership desk, doing child care, or assisting in other ways.

855. The International MOMS Club (Mothers Offering Mothers Support) caters specifically to at-home moms, whether first-timers or experienced, helping them connect with other women going through similar experiences. Membership is typically $15 to $30 per year but fees are waived for those with financial need: www.momsclub.org.

856. MOPS (Mothers of Preschoolers) International is a nondenominational Christian group that supports the spiritual needs of mothers. Meetings include a guest speaker and craft project for the moms while their preschool children participate in age-appropriate activities supervised by

a caregiver. The cost is typically $5 per meeting, but scholarships are available: www.mops.org.

more fun!

857. Find free music downloads for baby online: At www.ilovewavs.com, you can find songs for baby in their "For Kids" section. Or stream music in real-time from your computer at www.pandora.com (check out the classical *FREE* section for soothing music).

858. Sign up to receive a free circus ticket for your child from Ringling Brothers Barnum & Bailey Circus. Sign up before she turns one, and redeem the ticket later on when she is old enough to appreciate the circus. There is no *FREE* expiration date. Visit www.ringling.com and click on "Special Offers."

* PART EIGHT *

money—

keeping
more
and spending
less

family finances

budgeting

859. Make sure your family finances are in order, and enlist the help of qualified professionals. Let qualified tax advisors, investment professionals, and insurance brokers help you in your family financial planning.

860. Track your spending with your home computer. Most credit card companies and banks allow you to create automatic spending

reports online safely and securely. Mint.com is another online service that helps you manage your money, and is free of charge.

861. If you find that the free services mentioned in tip #860 above don't meet your needs, budgeting software like Quicken *WORTH IT* is a good investment.

862. Look for a low-interest credit card that rewards you for the purchases you make. Sites like www.billshrink.com compare different card options for you based on your credit, how much you spend, and which rewards you prefer.

863. Consolidate any credit card debt into a single, low-rate card. Make it your goal to pay your balance off every month if you're not doing so already to avoid paying interest charges.

864. Make savings automatic, but make sure you're getting paid interest. Online savings accounts like HSBC and ING often beat interest rates of traditional banks, plus there are no minimums or fees.

865. Apply for a social security number for your baby as soon as possible. You will need it when you file your taxes in order to claim your child as a dependent.

866. Don't forget to take advantage of the Child Tax Credit on your income tax return. Consult your tax professional to see if you qualify for other tax credits and deductions as well. Parents adopting children often qualify for additional credits.

867. Take advantage of compounding and save as much as possible for your

child early on. A $1,000 investment at age one with a 10 percent return will grow to nearly half a million dollars by the time your child reaches retirement age.

868. A custodial account is a savings account in your child's name over which you have control until he reaches legal adulthood. The benefit of opening up a savings account in your child's name is that the first $750 of interest is tax-free. The second $750 is taxed at your child's rate, which is almost always lower than your own tax rate.

869. Switch to a fifteen-year mortgage if you can afford to do so. Since a significant portion of your income goes to cover your mortgage expense, owning your home outright by the time your child enters college frees up those funds to be used on education. Additionally, by paying off your mortgage sooner you'll save on interest payments.

870. Refinancing your home may give you a little extra cash left over at the end of the month. To calculate whether or not it is wise for your situation, visit www.money.com and run the numbers through their refinancing calculator.

871. Don't invest your money in life insurance for your child. The purpose of life insurance is to cover lost income when someone dies so that the beneficiaries will have enough money to sustain their quality of life. Since your baby most likely doesn't earn anything, there's nothing to cover.

saving for college

872. Consider a 529 college savings plan for your child. It allows parents to set aside money for their child's education and let it grow tax-free. The federal government won't tax your money when you take it out of the account as long as it's used

for qualified education expenses. Often times, you can start with as little as $25.

873. A Coverdell Education Savings Account allows parents to contribute up to $2,000 per year towards their child's education. No taxes are ever due on the withdrawals as long as they are used for qualified education expenses. Unlike the 529 plan, Coverdell accounts may be used for qualifying K-12 expenses.

874. Roth IRA accounts can be used to save money for college. When you open up a Roth IRA, your contributions aren't tax-deductible, but grow tax-free until they're withdrawn. If you wait the required five-year period before making a withdrawal and use them for qualified higher education expenses, your earnings are tax-free.

875. Sign up for a Upromise account and earn money for college buying the things you would normally buy. Just use a registered credit card to make your purchases at Upromise merchants. Or, earn even more by using a Upromise credit card. To sign up for free, visit their website: www.upromise.com.

876. A painless way of saving money for your child's college fund is to collect all your spare change in a large jar or piggy bank. At the end of each year or on your child's birthday, take the money to the bank and deposit it in your child's savings account. You will be surprised how quickly all of that change adds up! To estimate how much cash you have in your jar, use the free calculator at www.coinstar.com.

* chapter 23 *

child care

babysitting

877. Join or start a babysitting co-op and trade babysitting hours with your friends. Not only do you get child care without any money changing hands, you're leaving your child in the care of someone you know well and who has experience with young children. (FREE)

878. Take advantage of relatives who offer to watch your kids. Not only do you get a break, your baby is creating a special bond with another family member close to them.

879. If you have a college or university close to you, post an ad for a babysitter on their bulletin board or through their employment service. Elementary Education students are looking both for experience with children and opportunities to make a little money.

880. Take advantage of online services that prescreen babysitters. Care.com, Sittercity.com, and Care4hire.com are just a few that run background checks on prospective caregivers for a small fee.

881. Barter for babysitting. College students may be interested in using your washing machine, borrowing your DVDs, or getting some free meals. Your neighbor may trade for lawn care, pet sitting, etc.

882. Day care centers and family child care are less costly than an in-home provider. Some even offer financial aid for those who qualify.

883. If your employer offers a flexible spending plan, allocate a portion of your earnings towards child care. These earnings are taken out pretax, which, depending on your tax rate, can give you a 20 to 30 percent discount on child care.

30% OFF

884. Be prompt when picking up your child from a day care center. Some child care providers charge up to $1 for every minute you're late. Coordinate your schedule with your partner so your child can be dropped off later or picked up earlier. Account for traffic and other delays when arranging a time to pick up your child.

885. Some places may allow you to help out with cleaning or making snacks or meals in exchange for a discount. It doesn't hurt to ask.

886. Split the cost of a nanny or baby-sitter with friends or neighbors who have children.

887. Through the Au Pair program, qualified foreign nationals live with a host

family and provide child care services for up to a year while also taking classes at a postsecondary school. In return, the host family helps with the au pair's education expenses. For more information on the au pair program, visit the U.S. Department of State's website at: http://www.exchanges.state.gov/education/jexchanges/private/aupair.htm.

staying home

888. After computing the cost of day care and expenses related to working full-time, you may discover you're not making as much money as you think. Run the numbers to make a well-informed decision about staying home with your child.

889. Besides day care, you will also be saving money on transportation, work apparel, dry cleaning, and lunches out if you stay home with your child. Be sure to think of every

work-related expense you will be saving and include it in your calculation.

890. Don't forget that you will be saving money on taxes if you stay home. Since most second incomes push families into a higher tax bracket, your first income will most likely be taxed at a lower rate.

891. Downgrade or give up one vehicle if you won't be using it to drive to work. Or, raise the deductible on your auto insurance. It may be possible for you and your spouse to share a vehicle if you're staying home with your children.

coupon
savings

coupon basics

892. Know when *not* to use coupons. You will need to become coupon-savvy in order to recognize when coupons are a good deal and when they're not. Coupons work best when they're combined with another deal or are doubled.

893. Carry a small calculator in your purse to help you calculate the price per unit when you're shopping. Most mobile phones have a calculator feature built-in. Be sure to make use of it.

894. Check the price on store-brand and private-label products first. In most cases, the store-brand version of what you're buying is cheaper than the more expensive counterpart even *with* a coupon.

895. Combine coupons with in-store sales and two-for-ones. A lot of grocery stores also offer "in store" coupons. Use your own coupons in addition to these to save even more. Websites that can help you pair discounts with coupons include:

* Couponmom.com—Offers a "Virtual Coupon Organizer" that lists grocery deals state-by-state and which coupons to pair them with for the best deals.

* Grocerygame.com—A subscription-based service that costs $10 for an eight-week membership. Subscribe to stores in your area and get a list that sorts discounts by percentage savings.

✳ Mommysavers.com—Members share the scoop on their local supermarket bargains and unadvertised specials, as well as which coupons they've paired them with in the Grocery Bargains discussion forum.

896. Find a store that will double your coupons. If your town doesn't have one, it may be worth a short drive to another town to a store that does. An Internet search using the keywords "double + coupons + your state" should yield a list of stores in your area that double coupons. Retailer Kmart runs periodic double coupon days. Sign up on their website to be notified and receive other offers via email: www.kmart.com.

WORTH IT

897. See if your supermarket has a limit on the value of coupons it will double (for example, most double coupons up to $1.00). If so, a $1.00 coupon is worth more than a $1.50 coupon.

898. Buy the smallest size. Most people are under the impression that you will save more by buying in bulk. When using a coupon, this usually isn't true. What you will need to consider is the price per ounce. Buying a smaller size for a $1.00 and getting $0.50 off will yield a greater percentage savings than using the same coupon on a $2.00 item. Keep a small calculator in your purse or coupon caddy to help calculate the best deal.

899. Start a coupon-trading group with women in your area. Let them know which items you need coupons for and offer to trade with them. To get started, email five to ten of your "thrifty" friends to see if they're interested. Have each friend list ten to twenty items that she always uses, and print out the lists. Keep the lists handy when you're clipping coupons, and then pass on the coupons to your friends. Or, trade coupons online. Visit the Mommysavers Forums to trade coupons with other parents: www.mommysavers.com.

900. Look for coupons in out-of-the-way places. Other places to look for coupons include in coupon bins at libraries and grocery stores, on product packaging, on the back of register receipts, in magazines (*All You* is a good one), and with product samples.

901. Print coupons at home. You can quickly and easily download coupons from manufacturer's websites and print them out. Or, find them on coupon sites like:

* www.coupons.com
* www.redplum.com
* www.smartsource.com
* www.afullcup.com

902. Join a coupon train. A coupon train is an envelope filled with nonexpired coupons that is sent between participants, or "riders"

of the train. A member receives the "train" in the mail and removes the coupons she can use. She then replaces those with coupons she has no use for and sends it on to the next "rider" on the mailing list. To join a train, visit the Mommysavers.com coupon forums.

903. It's important to note that paying for a coupon is illegal. However, paying for the time it takes someone to clip the coupon and mail it to you is not. Because of this loophole, dozens of websites as well as eBay sellers are offering their "services" to provide coupons to willing buyers at a price. Before joining a group like this, consider whether or not it's worth the expense and effort to get something that is typically available to you free of charge.

904. Make coupons easy to file, and easy to use. A large plastic index-card box or coupon caddy from the dollar store works well. Divide your coupons by categories such as canned

goods, baby products, cereal, baking, dairy, etc. After serious couponing for a few months, you will discover which categories work the best for you.

905. Put your coupons for diapers, formula, baby food, etc., in a separate envelope in your purse marked "Baby Coupons." That way, you always have them with you.

906. Always check your receipt to make sure that your purchases rang up correctly and that the coupons were properly credited. Many stores offer a cash-back discount on products that ring up incorrectly.

907. If you don't read the paper during the week, don't pay for the issues you're not reading. Many papers offer Sunday-only

subscriptions. Or, pick up the Sunday paper at the dollar store on Monday to save even more.

908. Visit your local newspaper on Monday morning and inquire about buying leftover Sunday papers at a discount. You can also ask the library to save coupon inserts for you.

909. Make sure you don't cut off the portion of the coupon that lists the expiration date. Many stores won't accept them if the date is missing.

online and high-tech resources

910. Avoid spending too much on impulse purchases at the grocery store by creating a shopping list—and sticking to it. Cozi .com is a great online tool to create grocery lists and have them wherever you go. Sign in to Cozi from any

smartphone to retrieve your list, or call their toll-free number to have it read to you or texted to your phone. Membership is free.

911. Twitter.com, the micro-blogging social networking site, can be used to find all sorts of samples, coupons, and discounts. Sign up to follow Mommysavers or other savvy bargain hunters to be connected with the latest deals: http://www.twitter.com/mommysavers.

912. Chances are you're already a Facebook member, or at least have heard about this social networking giant. Next time you're there, join the Mommysavers Fan Page on Facebook for recent news on bargains, freebies, and ways to live well for less: http://www.facebook.com/mommysavers.

913. Meetup.com can be used to connect with other thrifty moms in your area. It can be used to start a coupon-clipping club, collaborate on DIY projects, or organize a clothing swap.

914. Online coupon supplier www.coupons.com even has an application on the social networking site Facebook. Simply add the application, and they'll instantly provide you with a selection of coupons for everyday products.

915. Coupons are now available via the Internet and can be sent to your mobile phone. To redeem them, simply open the text message and present it to the cashier. Go to www.cellfire.com, answer some basic questions, and give them your cell phone number and email address. Participation is free but standard carrier fees will apply.

FREE

loyalty cards

916. Scan your loyalty card at coupon kiosks within the store. Shoppers at pharmacies like CVS and select supermarkets are now able to scan their loyalty cards to generate additional coupons and discounts. Discounts are based on past purchase history as well as additional unadvertised in-store specials.

917. When customers type in their loyalty card information online, they're eligible for additional discounts and coupons which are loaded onto their cards electronically. The discounts are then realized when the cashier scans the card and the eligible product at a subsequent store visit. These types of discounts are especially appealing because there's no clipping or organizing coupons involved. Shortcuts.com is one such portal for supermarkets like Kroger, Ralph's, Fry's, and more. Pgesaver.com

will load Procter & Gamble coupons on your loyalty card for you as well.

918. If you have an extensive collection of loyalty cards, consider consolidating all of the bar codes into just one card. Visit www.justoneclubcard.com, enter up to eight loyalty card barcodes and click the "create your card" button.

* PART NINE *

remembering your

baby

for years

to come

keepsakes and birth announcements

birth announcements

919. Photo card announcements are a quick and easy way to announce your baby's arrival. Before purchasing, always look for discount codes to use on your order. The Mommysavers.com Online Bargains forum has a listing of the best codes.

920. Visit Etsy.com to have a designer create a cute digital birth announcement

for you for $15 or less. You are purchasing the .jpg file, which you can then print at a discount photo retailer.

921. EBay is another source for custom-made birth announcements. Simply enter the search term "birth announcements" when you log on.

922. You can save a great deal by making your own baby announcements at home. Visit the Two Peas in a Bucket website for a wide range of ideas you can make yourself: www .twopeasinabucket.com.

923. Purchase a onesie for your baby and use fabric paint to write her birth statistics on it. Take photos of her wearing it to use as a birth announcement. Simply address and stamp the back of the photo and send it out as a postcard.

924. If you want an elegant announcement to place in your baby book, order a more expensive announcement for immediate family and close friends only. Send an email announcement to acquaintances and others in your circle of friends. What they really want to see is a photo of your little one!

journaling and keepsakes

925. The birth of a child is a perfect time to start a blog! Websites that offer free blogs include Blogger.com, Wordpress.com, TypePad.com, and LiveJournal.com. With very little technological know-how, you can upload photos and videos of your little one to keep family and friends updated. It's also an easy way to record daily events, special memories, and milestones your baby reaches. Both you and your child will treasure those memories as she grows older.

FREE

926. An easy and inexpensive way to create a baby book with your digital photos is to create a digital photo book. Most sites allow you to add your own titles, captions, and text; some will even import information from your blog. Upload your book in minutes, and you can order your own custom hardbound book at a reasonable price. Some sites offer discounts when you order multiple copies, which are great gifts for grandparents. Besides regular online photo processing sites, other notable websites include:

* www.mypublisher.com

* www.picaboo.com

* www.smilebooks.com

* www.blurb.com

927. Photoshop Elements is highly recommended photo-editing software great for bloggers and digital scrapbookers. It retails for around $90, but can often be found for less at

warehouse club stores. You can also download a free trial at Adobe.com.

928. If you're into digital scrapbooking, look for free fonts, graphics, and other downloads online instead of paying for them.

929. Have a scrapbooking party! There are all sorts of scrapbooking supplies available through at-home consultants like Creative Memories, Stampin' Up, and Once Upon a Family. They can be a fun way to get some of your friends together, learn some new techniques, and earn some free merchandise. To find a representative near you, visit them online:

* www.creativememories.com

* www.stampinup.com

* www.onceuponafamily.net

930. Take a photograph of your baby at the beginning of each month in the same type of clothes (such as jeans and a white T-shirt) in the same chair or next to a favorite stuffed animal. Or, use a special vintage outfit and photograph your child in it at each birthday. It is a great way to make a side-by-side comparison of how much your child has grown in relationship to something else.

931. Create a one-of-a-kind necklace, keychain, or bracelet with your baby's handprints or footprints using shrink film (Shrinky Dink plastic). Press baby's hand or foot onto an ink pad, and then the shrink film to create a print. Add lettering or additional graphics if desired. Finish according to directions on the package, leaving a hole to thread string. After the craft has cooled it can be strung to make necklaces, key chains, charms, or other keepsakes.

932. Be sure to keep the newspaper from the day your child was born. It is an inexpensive way to reflect upon what was going on in the world at that time. Add to the collection by saving a paper from each birthday, too.

933. A handprint book is a creative way to record baby's growth. Purchase a journal or notebook with unlined paper (such as a small scrapbook). On each page, write baby's age and use an inkpad to do her handprint. Add journal entries about what baby is doing at the moment and what she has recently learned.

934. Make your baby's handprint in clay at home for a fraction of the cost of a prepackaged kit. Mix one cup of baking soda, half a cup of cornstarch, one teaspoon of salt, and three-quarters of a cup of water. Heat the mixture over medium heat until boiling, then lower the heat and stir until thick.

Spread the mixture in a mold like a whipped topping container or margarine lid. When the mixture cools, press your baby's hand into the dough to form a hand-print. String it with a pink or blue ribbon and use a toothpick to write the date before it dries.

935. Stores like Michael's, Jo-Ann Fabrics, and Hobby Lobby regularly run 40 percent off coupons in their weekly circular or in the newspaper. Use your savings to purchase high-quality scrapbooks, journals, picture frames, stickers, and calendars. Sign up for their mailing lists for additional discounts.

40% OFF

936. Create a stepping stone for your garden by mixing plaster of Paris in a pie plate and casting your child's handprint or footprint in it. Embellish it with polished stones, mosaic tiles, seashells, or other items.

937. Hate to throw out or get rid of your baby's cute infant outfits? Create a blanket made from squares of your favorite baby outfits. It is sure to be a cherished heirloom for years to come.

REUSE

938. Another inexpensive keepsake is a baby's first year calendar. You can make one at home using a regular calendar or custom-make one on your computer. In each daily square, jot down a comment about your baby that day. Your comments can range from very ordinary (e.g., Nicholas loved playing peek-a-boo today) to a significant milestone (e.g., Emma took her first steps today!).

939. Receive a free congratulatory note from the president for the birth of your child: http://www.govspot.com /ask/cardpresident.htm.

FREE

940. Baby Anbesol has a chart to keep track of your baby's teeth and when they come in. Just visit their website, print the chart, and keep it in your baby book. The chart also lists when each tooth typically erupts: www.anbesol.com.

941. Bring a blank journal to your baby shower. Pass it around and ask each guest to write down his or her best parenting tips and advice.

* chapter 26 *
recording memories of your baby

taking photos at home

942. Take your own portrait photos using a sheet as a backdrop and some simple props. Use props that don't distract from the subject: a few strands of pearl beads, a metal washtub, fresh flowers, a ball or a teddy bear, some tulle, a wagon, or antique toys all add appeal to your photos without distracting.

943. Give your baby a piece of tape to play with while taking his photo. It will distract him long enough to take a few cute shots, and position his fingers where you want them.

944. Take advantage of new customer promotions offered by photo printing sites. In many cases, you get your first set of prints developed free. These websites also allow friends and family to print or download the pictures to use themselves:

* www.snapfish.com

* www.shutterfly.com

* www.clarkcolor.com

* www.winkflash.com

* www.kodakgallery.com

* www.yorkphoto.com

945. Visit the Mommysavers Online Bargains forum to see which offers are available.

946. Edit for free. Kodak Easy Share is a free software program with basic editing options and some creative features. It allows even beginning photo editors to create custom cards, album pages, and invitations. Click on "Kodak Store" and "Software" for a free download: www.kodak.com.

FREE

947. Your photos will look best with natural lighting. Position your subject in natural daylight if at all possible. When shooting outdoors, use filtered light as opposed to harsh bright sunlight that casts blotchy shadows and makes your baby squint.

948. Look for inexpensive picture frames at your local dollar store. Wooden ones are great because you can paint them with inexpensive craft paint to match your décor.

professional photographs

949. Contact your local university or community college to see if they offer a photography major and can put you in touch with a student who would be willing to photograph your child.

950. You may be able to barter for a photo session with someone you know who has a good camera and possesses good photography skills. This can not only save you money, but your child will probably be more comfortable with someone he knows which will make things easier.

951. Keep notes on certain poses, backgrounds, or props you like. Most discount portrait studios can duplicate what you like fairly well. Most studios will supply the props for you, but a teddy bear or special stuffed animal brought from home may add a special sentiment to your photograph.

952. Schedule your child's photograph for a time when she's well rested and typically in a good mood. Wait until you're at the studio to get her dressed, and bring along an extra change of clothes just in case you need them. If your child is prone to drooling, make sure she wears a bib until the last second to avoid a wet neckline.

953. Your success at a discount photography studio often depends on who is taking the photos. Ask your friends with kids if they can recommend a specific photographer, and schedule your appointment with him or her.

954. Never buy a photo from Sears, JCPenney, Wal-Mart, or Target without a coupon. Go online to search for the best ones before you book your appointment.

* www.searsportrait.com

* www.jcpportraits.com

* www.targetportraits.com

* www.pictureme.com

955. The best deal at most discount portrait studios is a one-pose package special, in which you get dozens of different sizes of photos for one low price. The key to saving money is to say no to the additional poses they're required to take and buy the package only. You can always come back later if you want a variety of shots.

956. Be prepared to say no to the extra (yet very cute) pictures the portrait studio prints up and tries to sell you when you pick up your portrait package.

957. When you get your wallet-sized portraits back from a discount portrait studio, most come with white edges. Cut the white edges off and finish with a corner rounder. It creates a more finished appearance and gives your photos a professional look.

digital cameras and camcorders

958. Contact local camera shops or newspaper photographers to see if they are interested in selling any of their cameras. Such places are always upgrading their equipment to include the most state-of-the-art camera equipment and their cast-offs are usually in pretty good shape.

959. Sometimes you can find refurbished cameras at considerable savings at camera shops. Most also come with a warranty and an option for buying an extended warranty, so you don't need to be hesitant about buying one.

960. The optical zoom is more important than the digital zoom. Digital zoom gives the appearance of a close-up image without the quality of optical zoom.

961. Make sure the camera you buy comes with rechargeable batteries. If it doesn't, invest in rechargeable batteries.

WORTH IT

962. You probably won't need any more than three to four megapixels, so don't pay for what you don't need. A four-megapixel

camera produces great 4 x 6 prints and enlargements up to 11 x 14 without compromising quality.

963. Be aware that your camera will not likely come with enough storage space and you will need to buy an additional memory card to hold your photos. Also, make sure your camera comes with a USB cord or dock that can attach directly to your computer or photo printer. Otherwise you will have to purchase a separate memory card reader.

964. Don't forget to burn the photos you want to archive onto a CD or store them on a jump drive for easy storage.

965. Instead of printing digital photos at home, have them printed through online photo retailers or at a discount store. If you're having 4 x 6 images made, it costs more in printer ink

and paper to do it at home. You can even upload your photos to their website and pick them up in-store to avoid the shipping costs.

966. Although not comparable to a camcorder or a digital video recorder, using the video feature on a digital camera may be all you need to capture a few moments in film. Consider how much you will really be using it. If you're only going to pull it out for baby's first steps, you'll probably be fine using the video feature on your digital camera if it has one.

967. Springtime is a good time to purchase a camcorder. That's when the new models are introduced and older inventory is liquidated. Never purchase a camcorder that's just come onto the market. Wait a few months until its price has been reduced.

968. Purchase a digital video recorder if you can afford to do so. Just like VHS tapes, analog video is quickly becoming obsolete. Digital cameras feature better picture quality, allow you to edit your videos on your home computer, and their batteries have a longer running time. The average home user can get by with a low-to-mid-range model that costs under $500.

969. When buying a digital camcorder, look for at least a 10x optical zoom lens and image stabilization.

special occasions

first birthday

970. Try making your baby's birthday cake yourself. An Internet search will yield dozens of sites with specific instructions on how to make the cake of your choice. Making cupcakes is even easier.

971. Check with your local supermarkets to see if they offer a free first birthday cake for your child. Many offer a free *FREE* sheet cake or small cake for baby if a larger one is purchased.

972. Parents can't wait to commemorate their child's first birthday with a celebration. Unlike the birthdays to come, this party is really more for you. Resist the urge to go overboard. Keep the guest list small. At this age, your child will become easily overwhelmed with a large group and experience sensory overload.

973. The focus of the first birthday party should be on creating special memories of the event rather than on expensive decorations, food, and party favors. Invest your time in ideas that will help make your celebration fun and memorable.

974. Have a cake and ice cream only birthday party. Let your guests know what you'll be serving so they can eat beforehand. You'll save big by not having to make a meal for your guests.

975. Start a "birthday tablecloth" for your child. Have guests sign the tablecloth, noting their favorite memory of your child from the past year. You can also do your child's handprints on it with an ink pad. Be sure to date each entry. Over a period of time your child will have a wonderful keepsake.

976. Instead of having guests bring your baby a gift, have everyone bring an item for a time capsule that the birthday child can open when he is older. Items could be a photo of the guest with the birthday child, a current newspaper or magazine, a grocery receipt or ad, etc.

977. Look at the dollar store for decorations. You will often find liquidated merchandise from more expensive party stores there. Frequently you can find the same themes and characters you're after.

978. Mylar helium balloons, which can run up to $5 at party stores, can often be found at the dollar store. Mylar balloons can also be saved and refilled with helium when you want to use them again.

REUSE

979. Instead of more toys, ask relatives who will be giving gifts to make a contribution to your child's savings account. Take advantage of the fact that your child doesn't realize it is her birthday. At this age, your child won't miss out on anything. By age two or three she will come to expect more in the way of gifts.

WORTH IT

980. Plant a tree on your baby's first birthday. Take a picture of him next to the tree each year to record both his growth and the tree's growth.

981. Start a birthday scrapbook. Include photos of the birthday child and her guests, the cake, and decorations. Have each guest sign the book and add a favorite memory of the birthday child. Include a copy of the invitation and jot some notes about what you did and what gifts your child received.

baptism

982. Most department stores carry baptism gowns and suits for babies, which typically run $40 to $75 on up. Be sure to check off-price retailers that stock many of the same items as department stores, such as Ross, Marshalls, and T.J. Maxx. You may find the same thing at considerable savings. Wal-Mart also has baptism and christening outfits.

983. Consider buying something that can be worn by either gender, so you can save it and use it for all your kids.

984. If you sew, make your baby's baptism gown out of your wedding dress train. It is a special way to reuse something that was very special to you at one time, and leaves your dress intact if you want to pass it on to a daughter someday.

Christmas

985. Each year at Christmas time, buy a charm to sew onto your baby's stocking. The first year may be a baby bottle, a rattle, or teddy bear. Each year you can add to the collection by adding a charm that has something to do with your child's year.

986. Use extra wallet photos or snapshots of your child as gift tags. Just punch a hole in the corner, and write to and from on the back.

987. It is hard to resist buying a "Baby's First Christmas" ornament for your child. However, if you wait until after Christmas to buy it, you can save up to 75 percent or more. You will still have it in years to come to remember the *75% OFF* first Christmas by.

988. Start the tradition of making an ornament for each child at Christmas time. Write your child's name and the year on the ornament as a lasting keepsake.

989. Don't spend your money on photos of your child with Santa at the mall. Most are of poor quality and quite expensive. If you ask, many Santas will allow you to take a snapshot with your own camera.

FREE

990. Take advantage of your baby not knowing about presents yet and save money by wrapping up things you would buy anyway. A young child will be perfectly happy opening up clothes, diapers, wipes, baby food, or maybe fun toddler snacks you normally wouldn't buy. Take the money you're saving on gifts and make a contribution to his savings account or 529 plan.

halloween

991. Search for Halloween costumes on eBay. Begin your search early enough to allow sufficient time for shipping.

992. Thrift stores are great places to find either complete costumes, or to look for pieces to assemble one of your own.

993. Costumes can be made at home with hooded sweat suits, sleepers, or other items you may have in your home already. *REUSE* Many of them require no sewing, and very little time.

994. DALMATIAN—For an inexpensive dalmatian costume, buy a white hooded sweat suit and add spots using black felt and glue. Cut the spots accordingly, and adhere them with tacky glue. Since the glue is washable, you can peel off the spots when you're done and use the suit again. Cut out ears and pin them on the hood with a safety pin. Add a black nose with a little makeup.

995. MOUSE—To make a mouse costume, start with a hooded gray sweatshirt and sweatpants. Make ears out of gray and pink felt, then sew or pin them onto the hood. Take a gray tube sock and fill it with newspaper or fiberfill to make a tail. Paint on a pink nose with a little lipstick and draw whiskers on with a little black eyeliner.

996. GHOST—For small children under three feet tall, take a white pillowcase and cut holes for the eyes and arms. Have them wear a white long-sleeved shirt underneath, and you have a cute ghost costume.

997. LADYBUG—For this costume, you'll need a black shirt and leggings, pipe cleaners, small pom-poms, and two pieces of red felt. Using a plate, trace a large circle on the felt and paint black dots on it using a permanent marker or black fabric paint. Cut the felt in half for the wings

and attach them to the back of your child's shirt with safety pins. The antennae are made with black pipe cleaners attached to a headband (add two pom-poms on the end).

998. PEAS IN A POD—If you have multiples, convert your double stroller into a peapod by covering it with a green sheet (take an old white sheet and dye it with fabric dye). Cut out a strip long enough to reveal your twins (or triplets!) dressed in green sleepers.

999. BUMBLEBEE—Use tacky glue to adhere one-and-a-half-inch black strips of felt to a yellow onesie, sleeper, or shirt. Use pipe cleaners attached to a headband for antennae, and hot-glue a pom-pom to each end.

1000. FLOWER—Create a flower costume with a green sweatshirt and a bunch of artificial flowers purchased at your dollar store or discount outlet. Cut the flowers apart and hot-glue them to a hat, and glue the leaves to the collar of the sweat suit.

1001. CHICKEN—Pair a white turtleneck with yellow tights for a cute chicken costume. Add white feathers from a boa and use yellow kitchen gloves for the feet and hands. The chicken's head can be made from a white cap adding red felt as the comb to the part that ties under the chin.

1002. PUMPKIN—Starting with an orange sweat suit (use fabric dye if you can't find one), add black felt for the triangle jack-o-lantern face on your child's torso. A green hat can be used for the stem, adding some artificial leaves with tacky glue.

1003. SKUNK—This costume can be made in minutes by dressing your child in a black hooded sweat suit. Add black gloves, stuff a small black sock for the tail, and attach masking tape down the back for the skunk's stripe.

1004. SCARECROW—A simple flannel shirt and overalls is transformed into an adorable scarecrow costume. Add a little straw peeking out of the sleeves, add flannel patches to the overalls with tacky glue, and have your child wear a straw hat. Look for a decorative bird in the artificial floral department to add to the hat.

1005. BLACK CAT—Similar to the skunk costume, this uses a black sweat suit. Add black gloves, stuff one side of a pair of black tights for the tail, and add ears to the hood with black felt. Eyeliner can be used to draw a nose and whiskers on your child's cheeks.

Easter

1006. After-Easter sales are a good time to stock up on dressy apparel for you child. Try to anticipate what lightweight coats, shoes, dresses, and suits he or she will need for the coming year and buy ahead.

1007. Check to see if there are free Easter activities in your area. Often there are events at the library or a city park, including Easter egg hunts which are fun for toddlers and older siblings.

FREE

1008. Items to fill your child's Easter basket can be found at the dollar store. You can also use this as an opportunity to buy things your child needs anyway, such as a swimming suit, sandals and sunscreen for summer, bubbles, or batteries for toys.

1009. You can often find cute stuffed animals on clearance after Easter for 50 to 75 percent off. It's a great time to purchase stocking stuffers or party favors for the year ahead.

50% OFF

tips for traveling with baby

1010. When you travel with an older baby who may be eating snacks in a car seat, be sure to put down a sheet on the floor of your vehicle. It will make cleanup much easier, and preserve the flooring of your car.

1011. Children under two fly free if you carry them on your lap. To keep your child restrained while in flight, consider wearing a front-pack or baby carrier.

FREE

1012. Look for flights that aren't full to increase your odds of getting an empty seat next to you for your infant. Monday afternoon to Thursday morning flights are typically considered off-peak and planes are less likely to be completely booked. You're also more likely to get a deal on your tickets if flying off-peak.

1013. In most cases, you can reserve your seat assignment online before you arrive at the airport. Try to book a seat with an empty one next to it. Or, arrive at the airport early to request special seating if available.

1014. If you do book a seat for your child, be sure to enroll her in a frequent flier program. Even infants can earn miles towards free flights.

contents

Published by Sourcebooks, Inc.
P.O. Box 4410, Naperville, Illinois 60567-4410
(630) 961-3900
Fax: (630) 961-2168
www.sourcebooks.com

Library of Congress Cataloging-in-Publication Data

Danger, Kimberly.
  The complete book of baby bargains : 1,000+ best ways to save money every
day / by Kimberly Danger.
    p. cm.
  Rev. ed. of: 1000 best baby bargains. c2005.
  1. Infants' supplies—Purchasing. 2. Consumer education. I. Danger,
Kimberly. 1000 best baby bargains. II. Title.
  RJ61.D227 2009
  649'.1220284—dc22

                            2009039224

        Printed and bound in the United States of America.
              VP 10 9 8 7 6 5 4 3 2 1

The Complete Book of baby bargains

1,000+ Best Ways to Save Money Every Day

Kimberly Danger

sourcebooks

"A quick, easy read packed with truly GREAT ideas, information, and suggestions."

"I am pregnant with my third child and this is still a wonderful resource to be used with every pregnancy, not just the first. I recommend this book to everyone who is trying to save money."

"I love it! I would recommend this to any parent, not just parents with babies. There are a lot of great frugal ideas in here that ANY parent could benefit from!"

"Great ideas for how to shop for maternity clothes that will last, homemade wash cloths and crafts for baby, and safety tips that will help ease your concerns."

"While many books told me all the things I'll need when our baby comes, I appreciated a book that told me what we wouldn't need! This book is super easy-to-read, broken down into easy-to-access topics/chapters, and full of easy-to-implement tips."

"My husband and I are on a tight budget right now and this book has been very helpful, especially for first-time parents."

"Every time I flip this book open I manage to find a few new ideas or am reminded of something that we should, or could, be doing to save money or help simplify my life as a busy stay-at-home mom! I highly recommend this book!"

what readers are saying

"If you want creative ways to save serious money, buy this book."

"A great resource for information on making your own baby products, extending the life of what you have, and how to get the best deals on new items."

"This book is an absolute must-have for mothers and mothers-to-be! Jam-packed with tons of money-saving ideas on what to buy, what not to buy, and where the best deals are."

"I have a nine-week-old daughter and this book has really proven to be a great resource on everything there is to know about saving money and being frugal now that I am a mom. I will definitely be including this book in baby-shower gifts in the future."

"If you are on a budget, this is the book to buy."